BEAUTY POTENTIAL

HOW FACIAL BEAUTY IS RETAINED OR LOST

T CARNEY BOWLES

T CARNEY BOWLES

For Vlada and Sasha.

Legal Disclaimer

The information provided in this book is for general educational and informational purposes only. It is not intended as a substitute for professional medical, orthodontic, or orthotropic advice, diagnosis, or treatment.

The author has made every effort to ensure the accuracy and reliability of the information presented in this book. However, the field of medicine, orthodontics, and orthotropics is constantly evolving, and new research may change the current understanding of the subject matter.

The content of this book is based on the author's knowledge, experience, and interpretation of available scientific evidence at the time of publication. However, individual cases may vary, and the information presented may not be applicable to all situations.

Readers must always consult with qualified healthcare professionals before making any decisions or taking any actions related to their health, orthodontic treatment, orthotropic treatment, or medical conditions. The author and publisher are not responsible for any adverse outcomes resulting from the use or misuse of the information contained in this book.

The book may contain descriptions of medical procedures, treatments, and orthodontic and orthotropic techniques. These descriptions are for informational purposes only and should not be attempted without proper training, supervision, and guidance from qualified professionals.

Any case studies, examples, or illustrations presented in the book are based on real or hypothetical situations. However, names, identifying details, and circumstances may have been changed to protect patient privacy and confidentiality.

The mention of specific products, services, or organizations does not imply endorsement by the author or publisher. Conversely, the omission of a particular product, service, or organization does not imply disapproval or criticism.

The author disclaims any liability, loss, or risk incurred as a consequence, directly or indirectly, of the use and application of any of the contents of this book.

Table of Contents

PART II: THE HEALTH QUADRANT: CHRONIC INFLAMMATION 105

HEALTH QUADRANT I: BREATHING (FURTHER READING) 114

How To Retain Facial Beauty

Our understanding of how facial beauty forms is entirely wrong. Most believe it's genetic; that faces are predetermined to look the way they look. This is inaccurate. In reality, faces are shaped by the forces that act on them, on our journey from babies to young adults, *after* we are born.

All babies have ideal facial proportions in their first months of life, because the womb's environmental forces are so consistent from one mother to the next. This beauty is either retained or lost by forces placed on the face as we grow into adulthood. The environments of the outside world are far more changeable and far less consistent than the womb's environment. And young, malleable facial bones are shaped by the forces placed on them. The outside environment causes most cute babies to turn into less attractive adults. Only a few retain all their beauty into adulthood.

Two quadrants define your levels of beauty and health: the Beauty Quadrant, and the Health Quadrant. When they are strong, beauty and health are retained. When they are weak, beauty and health are lost. These Quadrants are entwined. They support or undermine each other, preserving or corrupting your potentials.

Eight core environmental expectations shape the face. When they are applied as nature intended, environmental expectations are met, and the face will retain its proportions and its beauty potential. Beauty and health potentials are lost when the one or more of the tenets are consistently *unmet*. The order of each Quadrant tenet is weighted by its importance. Yet, all eight tenets are important, and all eight should be applied simultaneously, every day.

The Beauty Quadrant tenets are:

1. Mouth Posture
2. How You Eat
3. Swallowing
4. Body Posture

When mouth posture, swallowing, how we eat and body posture are applied correctly through our childhood, the face retains its beauty. The *Beauty Quadrant* shows the *direct* physical forces that shape the face. Consider these as correct form. These passive and active forces guide the face forwards and outwards.

When they are interfered with, the wrong kind of growth occurs; the upper and lower jaws become recessed, the face becomes thinner and vertically longer, the airway becomes squeezed smaller, and beauty potential is lost.

Ideal, natural growth causes the face to grow forwards and outwards. Compromised, unnatural growth causes the face to grow down and backwards, leaving the jaws smaller and set further back. This causes crooked teeth, impacted breathing and a less attractive face.

Apply all the Beauty Quadrant tenets consistently to retain beauty potential.

The *Health Quadrant* tenets are:

1. Breathing
2. What You Eat & When
3. Exercise
4. Vitamin D

These are the *indirect* forces which define how you *function*. A weak *Health Quadrant* impairs our ability to maintain good form of the *Beauty Quadrant*, and therefore strips away beauty potential alongside health potential.

Poor breathing affects mouth posture, as mouth breathers cannot maintain natural mouth posture. Poor diets cause inflammation throughout the body, which often induces unnatural mouth posture. Diets also impact how much you chew – as processed food is far softer that what we've evolved to expect. People who suffer from vertically grown faces tend to have weaker chewing muscles than those with proportional faces. Exercise both reduces inflammation and improves body posture. Vitamin D reduces inflammation, including, importantly, airway inflammation.

There is no magic bullet. No single easy fix. Instead, these eight environmental factors work in unison to retain beauty and health potentials. The tenets either support or damage each other, and there is huge cross-pollination between them. They work in unity when the tenets are optimal - creating a potential-fulfilling virtuous circle - or in abject disunity when they are suboptimal - creating a potential-destroying vicious circle. One weak link can make the other links crumble.

Poor function makes form worse and poor form makes function worse. If your respiratory system functions poorly and compels you to drop your mouth open to breathe, form is lost too, and ideal facial proportions can't be retained.

As an added layer of complexity, if a face doesn't grow proportionally, the respiratory system can become more easily compromised, as the upper airways become smaller, and are more prone to inflammation. A vicious circle is created which can be hard to break.

Beauty and health are symptoms of the Beauty & Health Quadrants being properly applied.

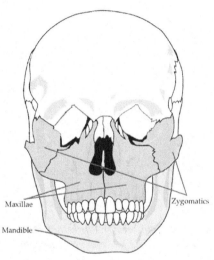

Figure 1 - The beauty bones of the face; the maxilla, the mandible (lower jaw) & the zygomatics (cheekbones).

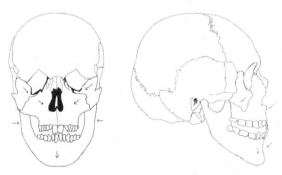

Figure 2 - Faces that grow wrongly grow longer, narrower and more recessed.

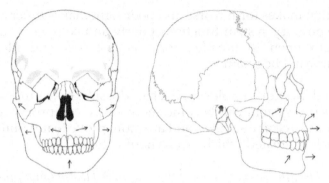

Figure 3 - Faces that grow as nature intended grow shorter, wider, and more forwards.

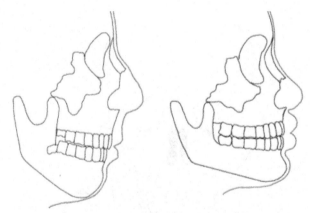

Figure 4 - Contrast of the profile and skull structure of a face that grows as nature doesn't intend (left) and a face that grows as nature intends (right).

The Two Facial U's

The face can be split into two sections that highlight where beauty potential is retained or lost. (See *Figure 5.*) This is represented by the two U's. These U's reveal how different facial forces affect different parts of the face.

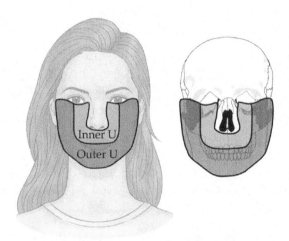

Figure 5 - The inner U & outer U of a face.

The inner U is the most important. It defines the growth of the maxilla, the most important bone for beauty. It's heavily affected by the position your tongue rests in your mouth. The outer U is affected by other parts of the Beauty Quadrant.

Many people have good outer U's and weaker inner U's. A few people have good inner U's and weaker outer U's. Most people have both a weak inner U and a weak outer U. It takes both to retain all your beauty potential.

Weak Inner U, Weak Outer U

When both the inner U and the outer U are weak, the face rotates clockwise, when you look at the profile of the right side of a face. This is caused by every aspect of the Beauty Quadrant being weak. There is no tongue support on the maxilla, so it falls down and backwards. Both upper and lower jaw recede. The face becomes longer and thinner.

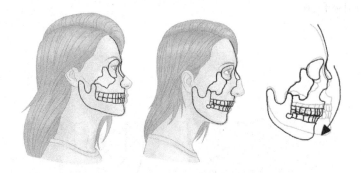

Figure 6 - A well-developed face (left), a poorly developed face (middle) & a comparison showing clockwise rotation as a poorly developed face drops down and falls back.

There are two ways the lower jaw can be weak. It can either recesses or protrude. Both are less healthy and less attractive.

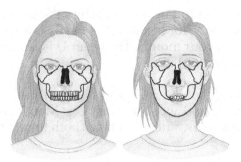

Figure 7 — Cheekbones are higher and wider, the dental arches are wider, and the maxilla and mandible are wider and vertically shorter in well-developed faces (left). Compare the facial bones with a poorly developed face (right).

Comparing a well-developed face with a poorly developed face highlights, for the inner U, the difference in maxilla width, forwards growth, width of the dental arches. Cheekbone projection and lower jaw width are displayed in the outer U. (See *Figure 7*.)

The other weakness that can form is an underbite. This is where the lower jaw grows too much and the maxilla grows too little. The cause of the lower jaw growth and the upper jaw recession is the tongue resting in the bottom of the mouth. This causes unnatural lower jaw growth. The tongue's aversion to resting on the palate, inside the upper dental arch, causes the upper jaw to be recessed, and smaller than it should be. Underbites are caused by unnatural mouth posture. (See *Figure 8.*)

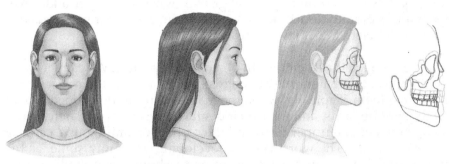

Figure 8 - Front and side profile of a face with an underbite (left & centre-left), the facial bones in profile (centre-right) and an overlay of an underbite (black) and a well-developed face (grey) (right).

In all cases of weak outer and inner U's, the maxilla is recessed and vertically longer, and the lower jaw is narrower and vertically longer.

Weak inner U, stronger outer U

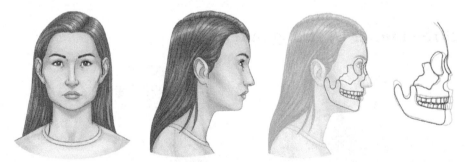

Figure 9 - A reasonably attractive face (left, center-left), an overlay of the facial bones (centre-right) and a comparison with a well-developed face (right).

Many people who are quite attractive have a strong outer U, but a weaker inner U. Their mouth posture is not perfect, but they keep their mouth shut. People who develop in this way tend to have a strong lower jaw. This is usually caused by bruxism – where people clench their jaws – or by lots of chewing. Driven people tend to have strong outer U's, as they literally grit their teeth and tackle life.

Typically, they retain reasonable forward growth of the maxilla. However, their upper dental arch is narrow, and their lower jaw is recessed in profile, but wide and well-defined when looking straight at their face. This occurs because they keep their mouth closed, but they don't keep their tongue on the roof of their mouth. The lower teeth stay inside the upper teeth, but both jaws don't grow forwards enough. The lower jaw is guided by upper jaw growth when the upper and lower teeth are habitually touching. A slightly deficient upper jaw leads to a slightly deficient lower jaw in these cases.

They leave a tell that their mouth posture isn't perfect. We can see inner U weakness, to greater or lesser degrees, by looking at the projection of the upper teeth. Typically, when the maxilla is underdeveloped, upper teeth point inwards, and the upper dental arch is narrow. There is also a gap between the upper teeth and the corners of smiling lips, causing a narrow smile. The worst case is developing a gummy smile, as the upper jaw drops down, causing gums to show when smiling. (See *Figure 10*.)

Figure 10 - A well-developed upper dental arch with straight teeth (left). A moderately narrow smile & inclined teeth (centre-left). A poorly developed, narrow upper dental arch with crooked, inclined teeth (center-right). A poorly developed upper dental arch, inclined teeth and gummy smile (right).

Strong inner U, strong outer U

People who have retained all their beauty potential have strong inner and outer U's. They conform to the Beauty Quadrant completely. They have forward-grown upper and lower jaws, great proportions, and they look beautiful.

Strong inner U, weak outer U

Strong inner U and weak outer U's occur when the maxilla quite forwards, but the lower jaw is slightly recessed. The difference can be subtle.

It's worth looking at the shift from subtle recession to obvious recession. When the outer U becomes longer, narrower and more recessed, the inner U becomes weaker too. The decline is obvious when we look at a side-by-side example. (See *Figure 11*.)

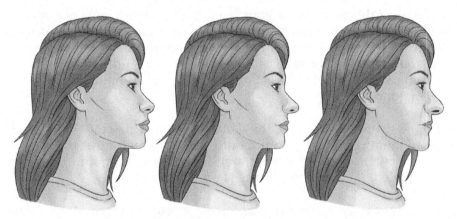

Figure 11 - Strong inner & outer U (left), strong inner U & slightly weak outer U (center), relatively strong inner U & weak outer U (right). The nose projects the same amount when we measure from forehead to nose tip in all of these, but jaw recession makes the nose look bigger (centre & left).

Beauty Quadrant I: Mouth Posture

"If the wind changes your face will stick like that"

A Quick Face Test

As you read this now, freeze your face. Don't change a thing about your facial posture. Don't move a muscle. Notice what your face is doing. Notice the position of your tongue in your mouth. Are your lips sealed? Are you breathing through your nose? Are your upper teeth lightly touching your lower teeth? Is your tongue pressed lightly against the roof of your mouth?

If you answered yes to all of these questions, you currently have good, natural mouth posture. If your mouth is open, your tongue isn't on the roof of your mouth, your teeth aren't aren't touching, and your lips aren't sealed, your mouth posture is unnatural.

Next time you are in a public place, look at people's faces. Most people today don't adopt proper mouth posture, most of the time. People-watching will reveal that those with open mouths tend to be less attractive than those with closed mouths. Natural resting mouth posture is fundamental for retaining beauty potential. Those who adopt unnatural mouth posture between birth and adulthood lose beauty and health potentials. Once you see it consistently in the world, you can't unsee it.

The Laws of Natural Mouth Posture

    Law 1: Suction your tongue against your palate and keep it there.
    Law 2: Keep your teeth lightly touching.
    Law 3: Keep your lips sealed.
    Law 4: Follow these laws whenever you aren't speaking or eating.

Law 1: Suction your tongue against your palate and keep it there

Your tongue should *live* in the roof of your mouth at rest. Crucially, it supports the inner U of the face. When a tongue habitually holds suction against the palate, the maxilla (the upper jaw) achieves forwards and lateral growth, and the teeth are nudged into their correct positions. The tongue acts as a support for the upper jaw, and as a barrier against the upper teeth so they don't tip back into your mouth. The tongue, suctioned against the roof of your mouth, stops the maxilla bone from falling inwards and downwards. (See *Figure 12*.)

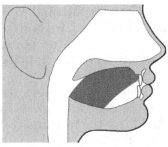

Figure 12 – Natural Mouth Posture. Tongue rests against the palate, teeth touch and lips are sealed.

The surface area of the tongue, when suctioned against the palate, expands slightly. This gives wider, more forward-grown jaws and a wider upper dental arch. Natural mouth posture supports the inner U of facial development and keeps the maxilla from dropping down and falling backwards.

If the upper jaw doesn't grow forwards and out to the sides, because the tongue doesn't offer around-the-clock support, it will instead grow downwards. When the tongue rests elsewhere in your mouth, its balancing force and support is lost. The upper jaw then shrinks, falls downwards and falls back into your face. (See *Figure 13*.)

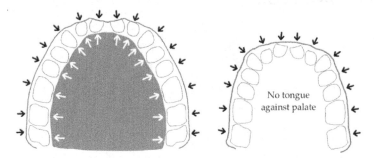

Figure 13 – Ideal, wide upper dental arch with tongue causes forces to work in synchronicity (right) and smaller, narrower palate without outwards tongue force & two teeth extracted due to crowding (left).

In the left image of *Figure 5*, we see the outward force of the tongue on the upper teeth and palate opposing the inward force of the lips and cheeks. In the right image, there is no tongue force which leaves the upper dental arch narrow and small, as the inward force from the lips and cheeks has no counterbalance from the tongue. This leads to an under-developed jaw, which will be less attractive, have less room for all the teeth, and will give less space for the airway behind it.

The upper jaw is dominant; the lower jaw follows its growth to retain lower-face proportions and beauty potential. When you hold unnatural mouth posture, the upper and lower jaws both recess downwards, and the lower jaw grows without the necessary guiding force of the maxilla – the central facial bone which holds the upper jaw.

When the tongue was positioned wrongly as someone grows, the maxilla doesn't grow wide or deep enough. Natural tongue posture is vital for the inner U. It holds up the face and it keeps the upper dental arch wide and deep. When the tongue habitually rests elsewhere, you see scalloping on the sides of it, and teeth that incline into the mouth. (See *Figure 14*.)

Tongues are never too big for mouths. Mouths can become too small for the tongue when unnatural mouth posture becomes a habit.

Figure 14 - A normal tongue (left) and a scalloped tongue (right), caused by a maxilla that didn't grow enough.

Teeth In the Maxilla

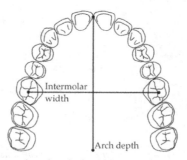

Figure 15 – The upper dental arch should be as wide and as deep as possible, to fit all teeth, including wisdom teeth.

A deep, wide upper dental arch allows room for all 16 upper teeth, including wisdom teeth, with space to spare. (See *Figure 15*.) When this occurs, all teeth emerge healthily and straight. This is what we see in the skulls of all our distant ancestors; brilliant sets of perfectly straight, fully erupted teeth, because they all naturally adhered to the Beauty Quadrant and the Health Quadrant.

The importance of the maxilla for beauty isn't fully lost on society. We care more about upper teeth being straight than lower teeth. Upper teeth are revealed with every smile and are held by the maxilla. However, most people underestimate the bone itself, which is where beauty is lost.

Modern dentists straighten teeth, but don't even consider the underlying maxilla bone which holds the upper teeth. The maxilla must grow forwards and outwards for beauty to be retained. Unfortunately, dentists often commit orthodontic butchery, removing the teeth and pulling the maxilla backwards.

When the maxilla doesn't grow forwards and laterally, teeth are crooked and there is not enough room for all of them. This means many people in the western world get their wisdom teeth removed. For some people who have worse facial development, a premolar from each side is often removed as well, to "make space" so braces can be affixed, and the teeth can be straightened.

The result is an upper jaw which is pulled back, a less attractive face, a recessed maxilla and a narrow upper dental arch, a vaulted palate, and breathing problems.

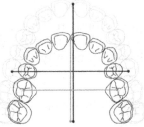

Figure 16 – Extractions, and lack of forward growth, cause the upper dental arch to become narrower and shorter. Ideal size (grey) & after extractions (black)

Having four teeth removed from the upper dental arch causes a mouth which lacks depth and width. In *Figure 16*, a premolar and a wisdom tooth has been removed from each side. This means 12 teeth exist where 16 should. Upper arch braces and extractions pull the whole maxilla backwards, not just the teeth, making the mouth smaller and the mid-face less attractive.

This has severe implications for mouth depth and width, and for how forwards and wide the maxilla grows. Braces, at best, limit and halt forwards and lateral growth. At worst, they reverse it. Lower braces act in the same negative way on the lower jaw.

We understand that fixed braces apply forces over time that move the teeth. Natural mouth posture does this too! But, unlike braces, you retain all your beauty potential and all of your teeth, when the tongue, touching upper and lower teeth, and sealed lips guide your jaws into their ideal positions.

The Tongue Shapes the Face

The tongue is not one muscle, as many assume, it's eight. And those 8 muscles are the most important muscles in your entire body for determining your beauty and your upper airway size. The tongue supports your face when it's properly positioned. Your maxilla is shaped by your tongue. Those with a wide, forward grown upper dental arch habitually keep their tongue pressed against their palate at rest and when sleeping.

Your tongue provides a forwards, outwards and upwards force - making your dental arch wider and pushing your maxilla forward. This foundation keeps ideal facial proportions intact. A short, wide, forward-grown face is functionally and aesthetically better that a long, thin, recessed face.

Where your tongue is positioned in your mouth, most of the time, dictates your bite. When the whole tongue covers the palate - at rest and during sleep - teeth will generally be straight and the face will generally be well-proportioned.

How Tongue Position Causes Malocclusion

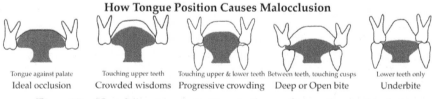

| Tongue against palate | Touching upper teeth | Touching upper & lower teeth | Between teeth, touching cusps | Lower teeth only |
| Ideal occlusion | Crowded wisdoms | Progressive crowding | Deep or Open bite | Underbite |

Figure 17 – How different tongue positions in the mouth cause faces and teeth to grow differently.

When the tongue is positioned wrongly in the mouth, malocclusions (tooth crookedness) and facial disproportions form. There are many ways to improperly position your tongue, and each causes a different malocclusion and facial disproportion. (See *Figure 17*.)

Crooked teeth are always evidence, and a symptom, of improper jaw development, caused by unnatural mouth posture. Most people's tongues habitually rest away from the palate, causing narrower dental arches, crooked teeth, and a more recessed maxilla and mandible. The exception to the rule is when the whole tongue rests between the bottom set of teeth and guides growth so the lower jaw is further forward than the upper jaw, forming an underbite.

There is only one way to properly position your tongue. It results in a forward grown maxilla and mandible, limits clockwise rotation, helps cheekbones to project upwards and outwards and gives you a strong jawline.

Where should the tongue rest?

The tongue should rest on your palate - at the top of your mouth. (See *Figure 18.*) The tip should be resting just behind your front teeth, but not touching them. The area you want the tip to rest against is the *incisive papilla*. Locating the incisive papilla is easy. Make the following sounds and note where the tip of the tongue touches the palate. "*La, na, da, ta.*"

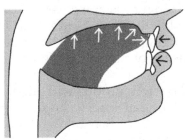

Figure 18 – The upwards and outwards tongue pressure when natural mouth posture is applied.

Place the tip where it makes contact with the palate, then use suction to press the rest of your tongue up, to fully cover the palate. You will feel the tongue spread to the sides. Once properly positioned, hold the suction pressure to the palate with the tongue.

Side Benefit One: Breathing is clearer when you apply tongue force against your palate. Place the tongue against your palate, ensure your upper and lower teeth are lightly touching and your lips are sealed. Then push your tongue quite hard and inhale through your nose. Your breathing will feel clearer.

Side Benefit Two: When you apply a suction hold long-term, the likelihood of developing a double chin decreases. Firmness from correct mouth posture will limit sagging under your chin (assuming you are within a healthy weight range.) A firm *submental* area - the space between the base of your chin and you neck - should negate saggy or hanging skin that can form there.

Law 2: Keep your teeth lightly touching

Your upper and lower teeth should be in light contact at rest. This acts as further support for the maxilla, and it affects the outer U of the face. More support from the tongue and lower teeth (and muscles of the lower jaw) means that the face can't grow vertically. Holding the lower jaw against the upper jaw stops downward growth. All growth, then, is channelled forwards and to the sides, retaining the proportions of beauty.

Law 3: Keep your lips sealed

Your lips should always be sealed at rest. The lips act as a counterbalance for the tongue - keeping teeth vertical. People who have good lip seal, but terrible tongue posture, tend to have teeth that tip inwards. The cheeks and lips push the teeth inwards, but the tongue doesn't push outwards to counteract that force.

People who thrust their tongue out without lip seal develop teeth which tip outwards. This can lead to an open bite, where the front upper and lower teeth can't touch. (Children who use pacifiers are also at a greater risk of an open bite and teeth tipping.)

When your tongue is in its ideal position and your teeth are lightly touching, close your lips for natural mouth posture.

Law 4: Obey these laws whenever you aren't talking or eating

These laws are necessary for optimal facial development. When you follow them to the letter from a very young age, your face will develop proportionally.

Even people who bring their lips together between sentences have better facial development than those who leave their mouths open.

When light tongue force is applied by your resting mouth posture, the sutures in your maxilla produce more bone, growing your face forward and outwards, rather than downwards. Sutures either hold different bones together, or occur within bones, like the maxilla. Pull the sutures apart and new bone grows at those suture lines. This is why the foundation of resting mouth posture is so important. Maxillary sutures can be nudged apart and they don't fuse until at least 14 years of age.[1] This is how forwards facial growth, and room for all of your teeth, is naturally achieved. (See *Figure 19*.)

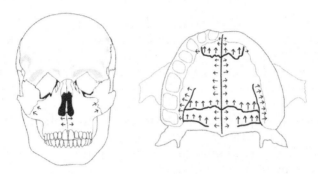

Figure 19 - How the maxilla grows laterally (and forwards) when natural mouth posture is applied (left). How the upper dental arch grows when natural mouth posture is applied (right).

Your genetic code has evolved expecting natural mouth posture to make your face to grow proportionally. This *environmental expectation* must be met, in order to fulfil your genetic potentials. Without proper mouth posture, your teeth, lower jaw, maxilla and cheekbones can't retain their correct proportions and they will droop, sag, grow vertically and become disproportional. The longer you can maintain mouth posture each day, the less beauty potential is lost.

Natural mouth posture is the most consistent facial force.

People whose mouth posture remains naturally placed and unmoving - as you check your emails, exercise, watch TV, and think - develop to have exceptional facial development. This is very rare. When our brain is busy, most of us grimace, or move our tongue, or fidget with our mouth posture. A blocked nose, and other symptoms of inflammation, cause us to lose natural mouth posture and open our mouths. The mouth-breathing habit can stick. While common, none of this is natural.

Overcoming Bad Mouth Posture Habits

It's very difficult to change unnatural mouth posture. We are often completely unaware of whether our mouths are open or closed. People won't tell you, because most modern people don't realise how negatively unnatural mouth posture affects the face.

Some people set alarms every 30 minutes to "check in" with their mouth posture. This may sound silly but keeping tabs and being conscious of it is the best way to correct poor mouth posture.

Children love to push boundaries. However, for their health, brain power and beauty potentials, no allowances should be made on mouth posture. A child should never leave their mouth hanging open. There are zero benefits of this. Teach children that, when they aren't talking or eating, mouths should always be closed.

Myofunctional therapy is a field designed to strengthen facial muscles to improve facial function and development. Myofunctional therapists focus in on where the tongue rests in the mouth. They instruct that it should live in the roof of your mouth.

Tongue Ties Can Halt Natural Mouth Posture

Tongue ties – skin under the bottom of the tongue that attaches to the floor of the mouth – can severely restrict tongue movement. It can affect breastfeeding for babies. However, it can also stop you from being able to suction hold your tongue to your palate. In that case, I strongly recommend a tongue tie operation.

Mouth Posture During Sleep

We have evolved to wake when the sun is shining and sleep in darkness when the air is cold. Babies in Scandinavian countries are placed outside, in cots, in freezing temperature. It causes them to breathe through their noses when they sleep, so the air is warmed, humidified and filtered by the nose.

When you sleep in artificially heated rooms, directly against our nature, mouth breathing is much more likely to occur. Heated bedrooms can cause us to sleep with open mouths. Even if your mouth posture is perfect for 16 hours per day, it can be awful for your 8 unconscious hours.

18

When we sleep, our mouths should be shut, and our tongues should be at rest on our palate. It took me months to train myself to do this. Applying mouth tape helps. When you use a strip of surgical tape in the middle of your lips, you can ensure that the lips stay together when you sleep.

Focus on mouth posture as you go to sleep and as you wake up. Go to sleep thinking about natural mouth posture until it becomes a new habit. I willed myself to learn over 6 months, with eventual success. Eventually, every time I woke up, I found that my mouth was shut, and my tongue was at rest in my palate. If you'd like a shortcut, visit my website for the best mouth tape and how to safely apply it.

Whenever you aren't talking or eating, shut your mouth and always maintain natural mouth posture.

Beauty Quadrant II: How to Eat...

Western culture is obsessed with food and dieting. Yet so little time is spent on *how* we eat. How we eat food - the speed, its hardness, our frequency of eating, the implements we use, and the amount of processing that takes place before it reaches our lips - is very important to our beauty potential.

How you eat protects or erodes your beauty potential.

How to eat is as important to facial development as *what to eat*. A parent should give their child hard, natural foods which require all the child's active mouth forces. Families who look unattractive eat in ways which don't utilise their active mouth forces. This deficiency chips away at their beauty potential consistently.

The active forces of how to eat start with food reaching your mouth and end with swallowing it:

1. Clamping/biting & tearing food
2. Chewing
3. Swallowing

We will discuss the first two of these in this chapter.

In today's world, virtually no one maximises their potential with active mouth forces.

Clamping/Biting & Tearing Food

We generally think that our bodies are fundamental and unchanging, whereas such things as table manners are superficial: we might change our manners from time-to-time, but we can't be changed by them. [Charles Loring] Brace [IV] turned this on its head. Our supposedly normal and natural overbite - this seemingly basic aspect of modern human anatomy - is actually a product of how we behave at the table.

- Consider the Fork: A History of How We Cook and Eat, Bee Wilson[1]

In most cases today, people use cutlery to eat. This removes several active forces on the mouth. Before cutlery, we picked up food and clamped down on it, then bit it and tore it using our jaw muscles, neck muscles and hand strength. Those forces are important for forwards growth.

Cutlery inhibits forward growth of the maxilla and mandible. When we used our hands, we'd grab meat, or vegetables in large chunks, then bite down and rip with our hands and teeth. Like how we eat pizza, but with far tougher food.

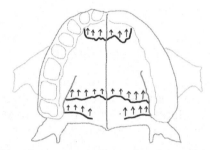

Figure 20 – Maxillary sutures in the upper palate and their growth when expected forces are applied.

When you clamp on meat then pull with your hands, the amount of forward force on your upper and lower jaws is incredible. It requires a lot of pulling, like a tug-of-war. This action, done with every bite, increases forward growth. Maxillary sutures are nudged apart by clamping and tearing food with jaws and hands, and by natural mouth posture. (See *Figure 20.*) This force strongly supports the inner U of the face, and the outer U of the clamped lower jaw.

The lack of this clamping and tearing force on the face during every modern, cutlery-served meal has consequences on facial development. Forward growth occurs from consistent passive pressure; the tongue pressing on the palate when proper mouth posture is maintained. It also occurs actively through movement - at mealtimes - by using hands and teeth to clamp and tear tough food into bite-sized chunks.

Figure 21 (overleaf) is an overlay of modern Swedish soldiers on an ancient skull. We can begin to see how much of an effect these changes have had on faces.

For facial development, forks serve no positive purpose.

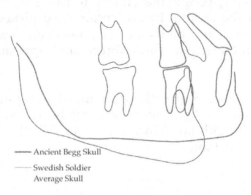

Figure 21 – Overlay of an ancient skull (black) and an average of 1,500 modern soldier skulls (grey). (Image courtesy of John Mew.)

Clamping and tearing food with your hands should be done evenly. When you pull the food from between your clamped jaws, pull directly outwards for the first clamp and tear, then go to your right side and pull outwards to the right, then go from your left side and pull outwards to the left. Repeat this cycle. This way you are encouraging your canines to expand your jaws forwards and laterally.

Eat Tough, Natural Foods

Children who break down tough food consistently are more likely to retain their beauty potential. This causes strength in the outer U of the face. Children who have some tough foods and some soft foods are likely lose beauty potential. Children who eat only soft foods are more likely to lose a lot of beauty potential. Children who drink all their calories through purees and soda will lose most beauty potential. Liquids/soft foods increase vulnerabilities. Hard, tough foods retain potentials.

As we have become more civilised, our food has become easier to eat. Most food is becoming softer. Cooking itself softens most ingredients. Bread, processed meats, even chewing gum are getting softer each decade. Canned foods are far softer and more processed than the natural ingredients used to make them. Our jaw muscles are woefully underused. The environmental expectations of natural eating are simply not being met.

Stone Age man chewed so much that their teeth wore down. The cusps of teeth, the sharp biting edges around each concave trench, became worn away. This is due to eating tough raw roots, plants, fruits, meat, nuts, etc. Our chewing activity is so much lower than the body requires to meet its potentials. We should dial it up significantly.

Our faces are becoming slimmer, flatter and longer. They are slimmer due to poor mouth posture and mouth breathing (inner U) and a lack of jaw strength (outer U). Strong lower jaws grow wider and keep vertical growth in check. Virtually everyone with incredibly long faces has weak, low-definition jaw muscles. Virtually everyone with short, forward-grown faces has defined, strong jaw muscles. Both upper and lower jaws are generally recessed in modern people. Tough foods help with forwards and lateral jaw development. Soft foods eaten consistently cause jaws to drop and fall back, and beauty potential to slip away.

Most food today, even tough meat, is cut into tiny chunks, sliced wafer-thin or processed heavily to make it softer and easier to eat. In 250,000 years of our *homo sapiens* history, this recent 250-year-old phenomenon has degraded facial development all over the world.

Eating Meat on The Bone

Almost universally, the toughest thing you can eat is animal flesh. Before we used forks or chopsticks, we used our hands. We'd grab a hunk of meat, bite down and rip pieces off to chew. This tearing force led to forward facial growth. Once in the mouth we would chew each tough mouthful until it was broken down.

Oftentimes, even the meat was raw:

> *"The hunger gratified by cooked meat eaten with a knife and fork is a different hunger from that which bolts down raw meat with the aid of hand, nail and tooth."*
>
> *- Grundrisse, Karl Marx[2]*

We forget that how we've eaten for the past six generations of cooked meals is dramatically different to the 11,000 generations that preceded them. Our collective memory is painfully short, and we live in an echo chamber of modernity. Eating raw meat, with hands, was common for over 99% of human history; and the forces applied, as Marx suggests, were significant.

Take a moment to think of the forces that would go through your hands, teeth and jaws when you clamp, tear, chew and swallow tough, beef. Doing so every day would transform neck strength, jaw strength, finger strength, and the growth of your maxilla and mandible as they are pulled forwards hard with each bite.

I recommend cooking a roasting joint of beef, cutting it into slabs that are 2-3 inches thick, then biting into it. It's very tough! It requires *force*. You clamp hard, then you tear hard. Then you must chew, chew, chew to properly break it down. Animal fat, in particular, can be chewed more than 50 times before it's ready to swallow. This covers all the bases of your active mouth forces; biting and clamping, tearing, chewing and swallowing.

The *clamp and tear* forces to tear a bite-sized mouthful from a slab of meat puts *significant* forward pressure on the upper and lower jaws that virtually no other food can provide. Tough meat provides most of the necessary active mouth forces that can retain beauty potential. Giving a child a big slab of beef, allowing them to use their hands, and making them take bites from the slab directly will result in the natural forces that a growing human should deal with to optimize facial development. Beauty potential will be enhanced by frequently giving children slabs of meat, eaten with their hands.

Chewing meat is easy to mimic with tough gum. The tearing action of eating tough food with your hands is more difficult to replicate. I recommend both eating tough meat with your hands and chewing tough gum.

How To Chew

1. Chew evenly on both sides of your mouth
2. Keep chewing until the food is liquified

People who have a preferred chewing side develop a larger chin on the opposing side. When studies tested this in twins, they discovered that this asymmetry is not hereditary, it's due to the habit of chewing on one preferred side.[3] To counteract this, chew evenly on both sides. You can get into this habit by counting – 5 chews on one side, 5 one the other. Eventually, the habit will stick, and you won't have to think about it.

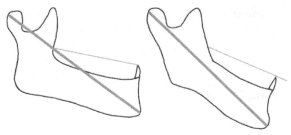

Figure 22 – Jaw length & space for teeth. Space for teeth gets smaller when jaws grow downwards (right). Lines are the same length on each jaw. (Image courtesy of John Mew.)

Keep chewing in this way until your food is liquified. It doesn't matter if it takes 30 chews to break down food. That's a good thing. Chewing in the right way, with tough foods, is vital. Strong facial muscles support natural mouth posture and forwards and lateral facial growth. When we don't chew enough, the lower jaw grows wrongly. (See *Figure 22.*)

Chewing & Tongue Exercises

For these exercises, use mastic gum. It's tough, natural gum from the Chios Island in Greece. It comes in little round drops called *'tears.'* Mastic gum gives more lower jaw strength and grows the masseter muscles on both sides of your lower jaw.

For the first exercise, place about 10 tears in your mouth and allow the gum to warm up. When it becomes soft, start chewing on your left side for 10 repetitions. Now move the gum to your right side and chew 10 times. Repeat this until your jaws get tired.

When you do this consistently, you can build up to 30 minutes a day. Men, in particular, can chew up to one hour per day. Consistently doing this exercise makes your jaw wider, and for men, more masculine. Women tend to not want such angular jaws, so should chew for 30 minutes a day.

You can also use mastic gum to strengthen the tongue. This works by flattening the gum against the palate with the tongue. Chew it 5 times on your left side. Then put it on your tongue and press hard against the palate just behind the incisive papilla. The goal is to flatten it, so it flattens backwards – moving the tongue so that as the gum gets flatter it goes further back on the palate.

Once you've flattened it, chew it 5 times on your right side. Then flatten again on your palate. Then chew 5 times on your left side and repeat the cycle.

A strong jaw and a strong tongue amplify the effects of natural mouth posture supporting the face.

Fast Eating vs Slow Eating

How quickly you eat gives clues about the environment that you came from. Did you eat as fast as possible and compromise the breakdown of your food and your swallowing action; or did you feel safe enough growing up to take your time?

One reason we learn to eat quickly is because of a danger. People stealing your food is a danger. This might lead to socially dominant people becoming better looking than socially submissive people, all other things being equal, because they have more time to chew and because their swallow isn't compromised. Another danger could be predators. A third reason we may eat quickly is how often food was available. When people are starving, they eat fast.

When you eat fast and swallow incorrectly as a habit, this is indicated on your face. The swallow mechanism quickly forms as a habit. Some claim, practise makes perfect. In reality, *practise makes permanent*. Only perfect practise makes perfect. Every time you eat, slow down. Ensure that your food is very well chewed evenly using both sides of your mouth, to protect against asymmetry and to ensure that your left and right masseter muscles are of equal strength and size. Then touch your teeth together before pressing your tongue up to the roof of your mouth as you swallow. Just as babies are perfect with their breastfeeding swallows, you should strive to be perfect with your adult swallow. This includes liquifying food before you think about swallowing it.

Fast eating can also cause temporomandibular disorder (TMD), where your jaw joints become overburdened and start to break down. TMD is far more prevalent in those with recessed jaws.

Mindful Eating

I was never one to buy into the process of careful, conscious eating. This may be a drawback that can be seen on my face. However, there is a lot to be learned from the ancient wisdom that has survived across millennia.

Here is a list of food habits espoused by Ayurveda:

- *Eat it fresh, ideally within 4 hours of preparation*
- *In a settled, harmonious environment free of distractions*
- *In a peaceful state of mind*
- *In a sitting position*
- *Only when you're hungry*
- *At a moderate pace*
- *At regular times*
- *Allow 2-3 hours between dinner and going to bed*
- *Only eat until two-thirds full*
- *Remain seated for a few minutes after completing your meal*
- *Swallow properly and slowly, using the method described in the next chapter*

This list doesn't include whether to use cutlery or not. Yet Ayurveda originated in India, where, even today, many people eat with their hands.

Eating slowly benefits digestion. There is no reason to chew or eat quickly unless a danger is present, or your hunger is so great. It is my contention that people who eat as quickly as possible are slightly more likely to lose beauty potential than those who can adhere to the tranquil environment recommended above. The *Theory of Propinquity* (in the *Beauty Is Contagious* chapter) suggests that our faces reveal our environments growing up, including our eating environments. Those with a more favourable environment, all other things being equal, have a better-proportioned face. This can be as simple as having better jawlines, due to maximising natural active mouth forces.

Could it be that a society competent in killing bigger animals achieves more forward growth, naturally? Ruminant animal flesh - such as cow, elk, deer and bison - is some of the toughest to clamp and tear. A Stone Age tribe who had the fitness and skill to chase, hunt and eat ruminant animals often would have optimal forward growth.

The Rules of How to Eat

1. Clamp and tear tough food when you bite into it.
2. Chew a lot before you swallow, evenly on both sides of your mouth, until the food is liquified.
3. Eat hard foods.
4. Swallow correctly (see next chapter).

This way, you get:

*   Forward growth
*   Strong masseter muscles
*   Hollow cheeks
*   Easier-to-digest food

This has a far greater effect on children. The good news is that most young children hate to use knives and forks. Eating with hands will be fun for them. Yet, more importantly, it will retain their beauty and health potentials.

Beauty Quadrant III: Swallowing

How Do You Swallow?

If you have a smartphone at hand, take a sip of water, move the glass away from your face, then film yourself swallowing. There is no trick here. This is a record of your normal swallowing action. Don't worry. You can delete the video after this chapter.

If your swallow contorts your face, you are swallowing incorrectly. (See *Figure 23.*) Your cheeks and lips are hijacking the process. The only active element in a correct swallow is your tongue.

Figure 23 - Unnatural swallow facial movements using lips and cheeks.

How to Swallow Correctly

The main difference between a natural swallow and an atypical swallow is the amount of movement on the face. Having a stoic face is ideal. A stoic face is completely still. For an atypical swallow, you will see movement in the cheeks and the lips. When you swallow naturally, all the work is done by the tongue. The lips and the cheeks should be as motionless as if you weren't swallowing at all.

The steps are simple:

1. Chew fully until the food is liquified.
2. Bring your teeth together & pause for two seconds.
3. Suck your tongue against the roof of your mouth.
4. Begin tongue pressure at the front of your palate, then push the rest against your palate hard and slowly.

Bring your teeth together and pause for two second to differentiate between chewing and swallowing. I rarely made this distinction growing up. I ate fast and sometimes swallowed half a mouthful, before continuing to chew the other half. An awful, unnatural habit. To stop this, you should pause. Take a moment to pause after your teeth are touching.

Create suction with the tongue and palate to get all the food between the tongue and your palate. This food should be well chewed and liquified.

The tip of the tongue should remain against the incisive papilla. Then naturally press the tongue hard against the roof of your mouth, and slowly swallow. That's the natural way to swallow.

Hard Swallowing Widens the Palate

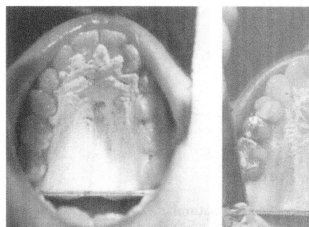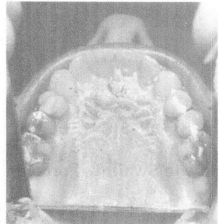

Figure 24 - Indicator paste placed on the palates of two subjects who were then asked to swallow three times. (Images courtesy of John Mew.)

Hard pressure of the tongue against the palate is necessary when we swallow. In *Figure 24*, the right patient has far less indicator paste on the palate after both patients swallowed three times, indicating lots more pressure between the tongue and the palate than the other patient (left). Notice how much wider the dental arch is of the patient who swallows with lots of tongue pressure against the palate. And there are two more teeth in the patient with the wide palate.

A slow, powerful natural swallow widens the maxilla, pushes it forwards, allows for a bigger nasal cavity for more efficient breathing, pushes cheekbones higher and wider, and makes the face more beautiful.

Swallow Check

Now, get your smartphone out and record this proper swallow. There should be no movement in your face, only in your throat. For most people, the difference between the first video you took at the start of this chapter and the second should be significant. This is how you should always swallow.

Drink through bottles with a thin neck. Cans, for me, are bad to drink out of while maintaining a proper swallow. Liquified food is far easier to channel in your mouth with pure tongue-palate suction, so ensure it's liquified first. Swallow after generating suction using only your tongue and your palate. Take small mouthfuls of food. Consistent big mouthfuls make swallowing without activating other facial muscles harder.

Every swallow of food or water you make for a month, should be done consciously. Be aware of taking your time and making sure that each swallow is performed properly. After a month, the habit should stick.

Beauty Quadrant IV: Body Posture

How Is Your Body Posture?

Your resting body posture - when standing or sitting - impacts facial development. People believe, generally, that their postures - both mouth and body - are better than they actually are. As soon as a camera lens is upon us, we tend to straighten up our posture. To honestly gauge your posture, either find candid photographs or videos of yourself when you didn't know you were being filmed, ask someone to take a photo of you when you don't expect it, or adopt your normal posture and take a standing and a sitting picture. Do it critically, i.e., don't straighten it up. Later in this chapter you will learn how to correct it.

How to Get Perfect Body Posture

Holding good posture should not be challenging for your muscles and joints. It shouldn't ache or hurt. You shouldn't feel strain from sitting or standing properly for extended periods. All babies and young children have fantastic posture. It's necessary to learn to sit up, stand and walk. Otherwise, they would forever lose balance and fall over. In the same way that beauty is lost through bad habits, perfect posture is lost through bad habits.

Those who believe that they are applying good posture, yet feel achy or strained, are not applying good posture. A caveat to this is those who have consistently applied poor posture, causing their body to compensate, making natural posture difficult to maintain.

The fundamental truth about good posture is that your bones take your weight, not your muscles. When your bones take your weight, your muscles support the bones through balance. This is highlighted by the extra weight your head exerts on the body when it's projected forwards. (See *Figure 25, overleaf.*)

When our muscles take our body weight, through improper posture, it affects our balance, our breathing, joints, tendons, organs, and the way our muscles and bones grow.

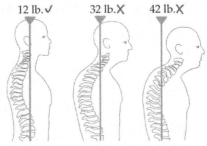

Figure 25 – Weight of head when different postures are applied.

The most important body alignment for beauty potential is the interaction between the head and the spine. The top vertebrae of the spine should not protrude too far forwards or curve too much.

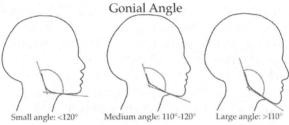

Figure 26 – The Gonial angle is the angle between the ramus (the more vertical part of the lower jaw) and the base of the mandible.

People who have a smaller angle between head and neck (measured by NSL/OPT angle) have shorter faces, more forward-grown jaws, and a more favourable lower jaw angle (gonial angle, see *Figure 26*). Those with a wider angle between head and neck have longer faces, more recessed jaws and a less favourable lower jaw angle.[1] (See *Figure 27*.)

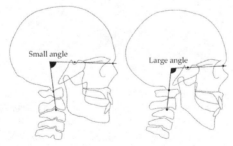

Figure 27 - Smaller NSL/OPT angle (left) promotes better facial development than wider angle (right)

A straight back and neck in relation to the head gives a smaller angle between the top two vertebrae of the spine and the skull. To achieve this, straighten your back, and keep your head facing directly forwards.

There are three planes of movement to consider with head position. (See *Figure 28*.)

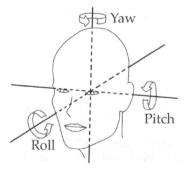

Figure 28 – The three planes of head movement.

The least significant is *yaw* - turning your head left or right when you look to your side. More significant is *roll* - tilting the head to one side like a confused dog. Tilting your head to the side adds weight, just as pushing it forwards does. It also causes asymmetry as you develop. Of course, the *pitch* of your head is most significant. Pushing your head forwards and curving the upper spine to raise your head - or dropping your head down to look at your feet (or smartphone) - is the hardest to correct.

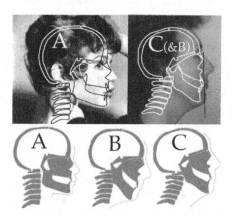

Figure 29 - 'A' shows natural posture of a beautiful woman (top left) and her skull and profile (bottom left). 'B' (bottom centre) shows what happens when unnatural posture is applied to the facial bones. 'C' (top right & bottom right) shows how people compensate by pitching the head up, so the face follows a vertical line. (Images courtesy of John Mew.)

Natural head alignment occurs when yaw, roll and pitch align, leaving your head straight, upright and looking directly forwards. This causes beauty potential to be retained. (See *Figure 29*.) As you scan the horizon the top quarter of your ear aligns with your eye. Imagine a straight, flat line running from your upper ear to your pupils. This imaginary line should run parallel with the ground.

Achieving Good Posture

The most important part of your body for good posture - standing or sitting - is your spine. The spine has three natural curves. The back of the neck is concave. The upper back is convex. The lower back is concave. The top of your spine should be directly above the bottom of it. The spine's curvature is natural and should be reflected in how you stand and sit. Your spine should be your primary focus when standing and sitting. Everything else will assume the correct position when you stand and sit properly.

Your body's alignment should mean that there is a vertical line from your ear that would drop to your anklebone, through your shoulders, hips and knees.

The second key is to ensure your shoulders are not hunched forwards. When shoulders *are* hunched forwards, the back of your hands face forwards like a gorilla. When your shoulders are aligned properly, your thumbs face forwards and your palms face inwards.

When the shoulders are pulled into the correct position, the chest opens. An open chest gives the lungs more room to breathe. Some people take this to the extreme and walk around with a pigeon-chest. This requires back and shoulder muscles to contract and leaves you unbalanced. The chest should face directly forwards, not slightly upwards.

Finally, never lean to the side. (See *Figure 30.*)

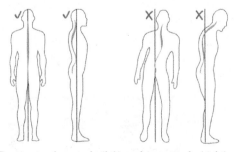

Figure 30 - How to stand properly (left) and improperly (right)

Wall Check for Standing Posture

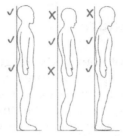

Figure 31 – Correct wall check posture (left) and incorrect wall postures (centre & right).

To correct your posture, stand with your back to the wall and move your heels about 6 inches from it. When your head, shoulders, back and bottom all touch the wall, you'll feel the correct alignment between your torso and head. (See *Figure 31.*) You should look directly forwards, so the top quarter of your ears is at the same level as your eyes. This is the correct vertical alignment that you should strive for.

Now, take a step away from the wall and maintain the same posture. This is natural, upright standing posture.

Sitting Posture

Sitting posture is as important as standing posture. The main priorities with sitting are to keep your back upright, as though your back is aligned against a wall, and keeping your ears lined up with your shoulders. This sitting posture requires you to keep your head looking straight, not down. (See *Figure 32.*) For people who use computers, you should either raise your screen to eye level, or point your eyes down without moving your head.

Figure 32 – Correct sitting posture (left) and incorrect sitting posture (right).

This body posture stops slouching. An upright back, keeping your head facing directly forwards, and keeping your ears in line with your shoulders, is optimal. From your waist, your legs should be bent at about 90 degrees, at your hips and your knees. Your feet should be flat on the floor, shoulder-width apart. No crossed legs, no putting your feet on tiptoes.

The best method for people who work at computers is to mix between sitting and standing desks. However, this might not be possible for everyone. Taking standing-breaks every hour is a good way to avoid slipping into bad posture. You can *reset* your posture every time you sit down.

Remember: Body posture and mouth posture are all part of the same reset. When you sit, straighten your head, push your tongue against your palate, close your mouth, seal your lips, straighten your spine, relax your shoulders, bend your knees and place your feet flat. All of this should be checked whenever you sit down.

Smartphones

Through our phones, we have the world at our fingertips. However, our posture, which should be upright and forward-facing, morphs into looking down towards our feet when we message and scroll. In times gone by, looking towards the ground was a sign of low status, lack of confidence and perhaps depression. Now, it's the natural by-product of consistently looking at smartphones.

There are two ways to avoid the smartphone slump. The first is abstinence. This is very effective but very difficult to maintain. The second is to keep your head facing forwards and moving your phone up and your eyes towards your phone. (See *Figure 33*.)

Figure 33 – Raise your smartphone for good posture (left). Don't hunch over to look at it (right).

Health Quadrant I: Breathing

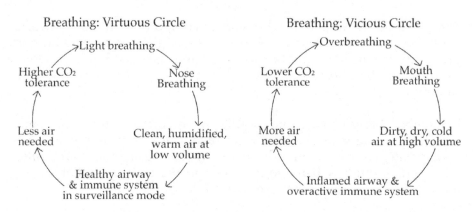

Figure 34 – The Virtuous Circle of breathing (left) and the vicious circle of breathing (right).

The two rules for healthy, natural breathing are:

Rule 1: *Always* breathe through your nose.
Rule 2: Breathe efficiently: Less air is better.

Exclusive nose breathing is vital to maintaining the Beauty and Health Quadrants. Never, ever mouth breathe. This goes hand-in-hand with the first tenet in the Beauty Quadrant – mouth posture – where you must keep your mouth shut whenever you aren't talking or eating.

Exclusive nose breathing filters, humidifies, warms, and controls how much air you breathe. These four things maintain a healthy, inflammation-free airway. Mouth breathing encourages breathing *more* air that's dirty, dry and cold. These four things can inflame the airway and cause chronic inflammation. Nose breathing covers the first rule. The second rule requires breathing exercises to train you to need less air to breathe more efficiently.

When we practice breathing exercises, our breathing becomes more efficient and healthier by increasing our CO_2 tolerance. Increased CO_2 tolerance gives us a bigger delay before we feel *air hunger* - a desire to take the next breath - allows for lighter breathing.

A lower breathing volume makes filtering, humidifying and warming air much more effective. Achieving this pushes your immune system closer to its optimal state – surveillance. It reduces snoring, increases

Oxygen transfer to cells, and relaxes you. We'll talk about how in the *Health Quadrant I: Breathing (Further Reading)* chapter. Now, onto the exercises.

A Quick Health Test – The Control Pause

There is a method to check your breathing health by measuring your body's efficiency with air. It's called a Control Pause.

To test your Control Pause, breathe normally, at rest, while seated for a minute. Keep your mouth shut throughout. Then gently exhale and hold your nose. The amount of time you can hold your nose without feeling the urge to breathe (*air hunger*) is your Control Pause number.

Set a timer and do this for yourself. Don't cheat: Take a breath when you first feel air hunger, not when you are desperate for a breath. On resumption of breathing, your breathing volume should be as low as before testing your Control Pause. If you are out of breath, you overdid it.

Keep a note of your score.

The best time of day to measure your Control Pause is first thing in the morning. Also do it before and after breathing exercises to keep track of your progress.

People who can comfortably sit after an exhale for 60 seconds or more have a far lower breathing volume than those who can only manage 20 seconds or less. A higher tolerance of CO_2 leads to lighter breathing and a lower tolerance of CO_2 leads to overbreathing.

How To Unblock Your Nose

When your nose is blocked, consistent nose breathing is impossible. Unblocking the nose is vital for mouth posture and healthy breathing. Humans have a natural reflex that clears the airway when we experience air hunger. We can take advantage of it to unblock our noses at will.

Unblock your nose is as follows:

1. Stand up and breathe a small, slow, silent breath in, and a small, slow, silent breath out through your nose.

2. Squeeze your nose shut with your fingers (and keep your mouth closed.)

3. Walk as many paces as possible you can, building up your air hunger.

4. When your air hunger is relatively strong, let go of your nose and breathe in steadily, slowly and silently. Your aim here is to keep your breathing as calm as possible. The first two breaths may be bigger than you'd like. By breath 3, you should be back to small, slow and silent breathing.

5. Breathe calmly for a minute or so.

6. Repeat these steps until your nose is completely unblocked.

Never breathe through your mouth here.

The Cheat Methods to Air Efficiency

The breathing exercises which follow are hard. Being in a state of air hunger is uncomfortable. The cheat method relies on a breathing device. When you trap your exhaled air, it's far higher in CO_2 than standard air. Breathing CO_2-rich air causes your tolerance to shoot up. Instead of having to hold your breath and struggle for air hunger with the following exercises, the easier option is breathing very slowly through the breathing device.

I have included the best breathing devices on my website. That said, you do not *need* to use a breathing device! Many people have seen excellent results simply by doing the exercises. Breathing devices are a shortcut, like using gym equipment instead of doing push ups. These devices are the only time that mouth breathing is ever acceptable.

The other cheats to ensure that you always breathe healthily, even when sleeping, are a chin strap or mouth tape to keep your mouth shut. These, too, can be found on my website.

Finally, you can also track your breathing practice through breathing apps. I list all the above online at:

http://tcarneybowles.com/breathing

You don't need to use them. You can do breathing exercises for free. These items and apps just offer faster results.

Exercise 1: Reduced Breathing

Reduced breathing is simply breathing so lightly and slowly that you feel mild air hunger. The goal is to maintain air hunger comfortably. This has obvious physiological effects. Your body relaxes, saliva is produced (the opposite of a dry-mouth stress response) and you increase CO_2 tolerance.

To do this exercise, you can either lay down or sit down. You can do this when you are watching TV, browsing the internet, or even working at your desk.

Remember, deep breathing is defined by how deeply into your body air goes (ideally down to the bottom of your lungs, pushing against your abdomen), not how much you breathe in! Modern society has confused deep breaths and big breaths. Big breaths promote a stress response and cause the air you inhale to be less filtered, warmed and humidified. The chest shouldn't expand. The abdomen should.

1. Breathe in deeply to your abdomen, slowly and silently.

2. Breathe out slowly and silently.

3. When you have the right technique, restrict your breaths so they are smaller, but go just as deep. Embrace mild air hunger. Keep focusing on only moving your abdomen.

4. Repeat for as long as you are comfortable.

To begin with, reduced breathing can be done for 5 minutes at a time. Aim for 40 minutes or more per day. Richard Brown and Patricia Gerberg - authors of *The Healing Power of the Breath: Simple Techniques to Reduce Stress and Anxiety, Enhance Concentration, and Balance Your Emotions* - found that 5.5 second inhales and 5.5 second exhales promote the best health. When you combine these timings with sipping in tiny amounts of air during reduced breathing, you begin to see profound benefits.

Exercise 2: Breathing During Movement

Breathing during movement - during housework, climbing stairs, or cooking for example - is very effective and so subtle that no one should ever notice.

1. Moderate your breathing so you have mild air hunger before you start moving.

2. Exhale and hold the exhale - don't inhale - for as long as is comfortable.

3. Gently breathe until you feel your normal breathing rate resume.

4. Take between 3-5 small, long, slow breaths.

5. Repeat from step 2.

This exercise is great for low-level activity. It is not supposed to feel strained. It's simply an opportunity to train your body to operate better on less air. If you are finding it too difficult, you are either not breathing enough air (at steps 1 & 3), or your exhale hold is too long (step 2).

Exercise 3: "High Altitude" Walking

Altitude training is effective for athletes because air pressure is far lower at higher altitude. This low pressure means that for every litre of air you inhale, there is less oxygen. Air molecules are more spaced out. When athletes train at altitude, the body becomes more efficient with oxygen. It creates more red blood cells, which carry more Oxygen, to compensate.

Training at high altitude, then competing at lower altitude increases performance. The thicker air supplies more Oxygen. This can be mimicked, to a certain extent, with breathing exercises.

Walk at a comfortable pace and make sure you are breathing through your nose. If you are breathing too heavily, slow down your walking pace.

1. Exhale and hold the exhale and take as many steps as is comfortable.

2. Gently inhale when you feel air hunger. Make sure you don't take a huge breath.

3. Take between 3-5 small, long, slow breaths.

4. Repeat from step 1.

You can also do this on a bicycle by counting rotations of the pedals. When swimming, you can extend the number of strokes between breaths. As your body slowly adapts, the number of steps, rotations or strokes will increase between the exhale and the inhale.

When you feel air hunger make sure you breathe. Don't push your body to a point where you may pass out!

Intense "High Altitude" Training

Once you are comfortably able to find a rhythm for exhales and exercise at low intensity, you can begin to use the same technique for higher intensity work. When you run, you can exhale and count the paces. At first you may struggle with 10. However, with practise, you can climb to 20, 30 or 50. The same is true on bicycles with the number of rotations your pedals complete. And when you swim, you could go from a breath between each stroke, to 5, 7 or 9.

The key is to not overextend. Your pace should be consistent. Don't sprint. Find your rhythm.

1. Exhale and hold the exhale and run as many paces as is comfortable.

2. Inhale when you feel air hunger. Try to control your breathing. Count your paces, rotations or strokes between each breath.

3. Take between 3-5 breaths.

4. Repeat from step 1.

When doing higher intensity exercise, you need to breathe deeper. However, your breathing should be steady. If you are too explosive or too fast, you will not be able to control your breathing. Consistent 30-minute workouts at a pace where you can manage your breathing in this way will mean that if you ever chose to breathe without pauses, your athletic performance will increase dramatically.

If you choose to count your movement between exhale and inhale (step 1), you will be able to track how much more efficient your body becomes.

Exercise 4: Breathing Recovery

After exercising your body needs to recover. Your brain also needs to recover when you are working hard or overthinking. This exercise helps with both.

1. Exhale through your nose.

2. Hold the exhale for between 3-5 seconds.

3. Breathe as normal for 1-2 breaths.

4. Repeat until you are calm.

Health Quadrant II: What to Eat

The Purpose of a Diet

A diet is only healthy when it *eliminates chronic inflammation* and facilitates *normal immunity*, where the immune system is in surveillance mode. Weight loss will follow. Feeling healthier will follow. When chronic inflammation is eliminated, the body has more scope to reach potentials and avoid vulnerabilities. Eating food that also requires lots of clamping, tearing and chewing, is even more beneficial.

> *Your diet becomes a liability when it provokes an immune response beyond normal immunity, irrespective of how healthy you believe it is.*

Writing solely about diet could fill a whole book. However, my message is to only eat things that cause no inflammation. Chronic inflammation causes a weak Health Quadrant, which can cause chronic respiratory issues (amongst many other side effects). When food causes mucus to form, blocking a child's nose, that child is forced to mouth breathe. This causes a habit to form that can destroy beauty potential, the loss of natural mouth posture.

Mouth breathing children are more likely to develop a weak swallow too, as the tongue doesn't touch the palate. Foods that cause inflammation are also more likely to be soft, which affects how much chewing is required. It's a vicious circle.

Food that inflames your body is not healthy food for you. It doesn't matter if it's fruit or vegetables. It doesn't matter if it's organic, wholegrain bread. It doesn't matter if the media tells you that the diet you eat is the healthiest diet! *Any* food that causes chronic inflammation is unhealthy for you.

Large food studies take an average of the diets that cause the least harm, and work best for the majority of people. You are not the majority of people. You are one person. All that matters to you is to eradicate any foods that inflame *you*.

We often eat the same meals, with the same ingredients, day after day. This can cause an inflammatory response to become chronic. Keep eating inflammatory foods, and you keep your body in a constant state of inflammation. Paradoxically, the advice we are given about eating a varied diet could curse us. If you are sensitive to five different food insults – say; gluten, lactose, nightshade vegetables, soy and eggs – and you continue to eat them, thinking that your diet is varied and therefore healthy, you are simply damaging yourself in five ways.

The Best Diet(s)

There are diets which are good for us all, we're told, while others are bad. This is true to some extent, but different people respond differently to certain "good" and "bad" foods. Some of us are highly sensitive to oxalates, others to dairy, others to lectins, or nuts, or shellfish, or refined sugar. People who say, *"Try the XYZ Diet because it worked for me,"* aren't considering the differences in food tolerances and gut microbiomes which shape our individual health potential.

While someone might thrive on a mainly vegan diet, someone else - with low tolerance to lectins found in many fruits and vegetables - may feel the most benefit from a more carnivorous diet. The differentiator is how an individual's immune system reacts to what you consume.

This is so important to retaining your beauty and health potentials that it bears repeating. There is no single perfect diet that works for everyone. Your perfect diet is one which returns your immune system to a constant state of normal immunity (which, by the way, can only truly occur in tandem with efficient breathing.) Any food which provokes a heightened immune response is inherently bad for you - it could be cheese, or beetroot, or even broccoli! Any food - no matter how "healthy" - which increases inflammation in your body is *bad for you!*

Let's say your child suffers from blocked noses, hay fever, asthma and skin conditions. You believe you feed then a healthy diet, rich in fruits and vegetables. Guess what? The diet is, in fact, very unhealthy for them! You may be certain that you are doing what's best. But this is misguided. Their diet is causing their immune system to be constantly inflamed. Continuing the diet continues inflammation. The result is that their Health Quadrant and their Beauty Quadrant are very weak. They are on a road to losing their potentials, and it will only get worse over time through an inflammatory cascade.

Have you ever discovered something new that you, or someone you love, suddenly became intolerant to? That's the inflammatory cascade in action. You must address and remove all triggers to the immune system ruthlessly. Your health depends on it.

Blood testing

Blood tests can reveal heightened antibodies in the blood. It isn't free, but it saves months of guesswork. Finding and eradicating inflammatory foods is vital to retaining beauty and health potentials.

Once you learn a food is inflammatory, completely avoid it. Anything that insults your immune response is dangerous to your health, directly, and your beauty potential, indirectly.

I recommend a few trusted intolerance tests on my website at tcarneybowles.com. There are others that are equally effective, but I can only vouch for those on my site.

Eat every type of food you ever eat before a test, so that there are inflammation markers in the blood. Then, when you get your results, you will know what you can and can't eat.

After your results, restructure your diet to only contain non-inflammatory foods.

If blood testing is outside your budget, don't worry. An elimination diet can reveal your inflammatory foods. It's just a far longer process.

Finding Intolerances & Healing the Gut - Elimination Diet

Elimination diets cut down the foods you eat. The goal is to eliminate any food that may cause inflammation, to return you to normal immunity, before adding those foods back, to figure out which specifically inflames you. You should consider an elimination diet if you suffer from any of the following: changes in your skin like rashes, psoriasis or eczema; headaches or migraines; fatigue; poor sleep; bloating; stomach cramps or pain; joint pain; unusual bowel movements; or changes in breathing.

General elimination diets remove the following:

Gluten, Dairy, Eggs, Soy, Fast Food, Alcohol, Seafood, Pork, Nuts, Nightshade vegetables, Corn

I recommend that you eliminate all gluten. While you may not be intolerant to gluten directly, it *always* causes gut permeability. This allows foods to break through the gut wall and into the bloodstream. If you are intolerant to any food that breaks through the gut wall, your immune system will attack it in the blood and cause collateral damage to healthy cells wherever that blood may flow. This is why your joints, gut, skin, brain, or seemingly unconnected places can be affected by inflammation.

I recommend just eating beef and salt if you are a meat-eater, or sweet potato and bananas if you are a vegetarian. After a week or two, you can add a new food back into your diet every 4 days. This way, you'll discover what causes inflammation in your body. After reintroducing a food, if there is no inflammation after 4 days, it's safe.

People who are highly sensitive to many foods have found solace in a carnivore diet. Red meat has no inflammatory effects, which is why the carnivore diet is proving so effective for those with autoimmune conditions. The long-term results of a completely carnivore diet is unknown. However, a Harvard study showed that:

> *"Contrary to common expectations, adults consuming a carnivore diet experienced few adverse effects and instead reported health benefits and high satisfaction."*[1]

Obesity

Being overweight itself causes chronic inflammation, as many parts of the body are under constant stress. People who eat more consume more triggering foods, put more stress on organs, and have less energy to repair the body as so much is expended on digesting food, and this alone can destroy health. Obesity causes swelling and pain. It also reduces facial beauty when a face becomes fat.

Reaching a healthy Body Mass Index will strengthen your Health Quadrant. It also increases beauty, both for the face and the body.

Health Quadrant II (Continued): When to Eat

Fasting Protocols

Warning: No fasting should be undertaken without medical supervision. Talk to your doctor before embarking on any fast.

Many people describe the following as diets. They are not diets in the strict sense. They are guidelines on when to eat. Their benefit is in the inflammation-fighting properties they possess – and they help with weight loss. Fasting could reduce inflammation because you are reducing the number of times your immune system may be challenged, and by allowing your body more time to heal, before pouring your energy into digestion with the next meal.

16/8

The 16/8 method of eating means that you restrict food for 16 hours each day. This 16 hour includes sleeping. The 8 hours represents your eating window. For many people, it simply requires that they skip breakfast. On a traditional 16/8 intermittent fasting regime, you can drink water, black coffee, and tea without milk. Zero calorie drinks are allowed. Stricter proponents of the diet might also restrict water for the 16-hour period.

Some people like to extend the fasting period and practise 20/4. A 20-hour fasting period and a 4-hour eating window.

5:2

The 5:2 diet is an eating plan where you eat normally for 5 days per week and restrict your calories to 500 (for women) and 600 (for men) for 2 days. The ease of this eating plan and the book and TV programme about it on the BBC made this quickly very popular.

Eat Stop Eat

Eat Stop Eat is like the 5:2 Diet, except you fast for 24 hours, two days per week. On this protocol, you are allowed to drink zero calorie tea, coffee and water.

Alternate Day Fasting

Alternate Day Fasting is like Eat Stop Eat, except you eat one day, then fast for 24 hours the next day, then eat normally, then fast for 24 hours again. Every alternate day requires a 24 hour fast.

I believe that this method should be used by people who are overweight, under medical supervision.

OMAD

OMAD stands for One Meal A Day. Typically, people who do OMAD eat once in a window of an hour or so. On a normal OMAD diet, you can drink calorie-free fluids - tea, coffee and water. Some like to dry fast between meals. Meaning that you drink in a specific window and eat in a specific window.

Longer Fasting

Longer fasting is something that many religions and cultures have embraced. I am reticent to give it too much consideration because of the major problem with eating disorders in modern society. People should eat a healthy amount of calories, of foods that don't inflame them.

Health Quadrant III: Exercise

Exercise reduces inflammation in everyone (unless you overexercise.) This is why it's the third tenet of the Health Quadrant. It also improves body posture and exercising your jaw muscles with mastic gum helps with natural mouth posture.

Running

Running, humanity's natural exercise, is fantastic for breathing, posture, fitness, and reducing inflammation. The most efficient way to run is to stand tall, to look directly ahead, to keep your back straight and your shoulders back. We lose natural running posture less, in general, than natural standing or sitting posture. If you run inefficiently, you will ache far more than you should, which teaches us to run more efficiently.

We can practice reduced breathing while running. First, by only breathing through the nose. And second, by restricting breathing between strides. Yet, running is a complex physiological feat. If we were to put it in terms of music, it's an orchestra. Wind instruments are our breathing. String instruments are our form and balance. Percussion instruments are our running rhythm. Only when they all work *in concert*, can you extract the most out of the exercise.

In *Born to Run*, Christopher McDougall talks about how the Tarahumara people ran. While popular culture focused on footwear and which part of the foot first contacts the ground with each stride, he said something just as significant: *"Before the Tarahumara run long, they get strong."*[1]

The Tarahumara live on steep hills. Hill running is weightlifting and speed running combined. Run up hill a lot and you are lifting your weight with each stride and training your body to run *fast* on flat terrain.

In 1971, physiologist Dale Groom wrote a paper on the Tarahumara. He measured their heart rates and blood pressure before, during and after a 5-hour race. He found that the average heart rate was 130 beats per minute. Most runners in a marathon reach *180* beats per minute! Groom found their physical performance so unexpected that he was moved to say:

"Probably not since the days of the ancient Spartans has a people achieved such a high state of physical conditioning."[2]

When they finished the race, they didn't pant or struggle to regain normal composure. They were composed, chatting to each other like a family walking through a park.

"Almost unbelievable is the pulmonary performance of these runners who, after running competitively for hours, cross the finish line and stand quietly without panting while one examines them, seemingly unperturbed by the effort."[3]

Training for a trail run on a running track isn't going to prepare your body for the variations in surface, elevation, inclines and declines, decisions on where to place each stride, stride-length, etc.

Adaptability is the premise of trail-running successfully. It's also the premise of successfully retaining your potentials. The ability to prosper in many different environments is the cornerstone of retaining potentials. The challenge of trail running reflects the far larger challenge of our development from birth to adulthood. You must be fit, strong, balanced, resilient, have a healthy diet, breathe efficiently, maintain natural posture and be consistent. Running outside also exposes you to Vitamin D, the final Health Quadrant tenet.

Swimming

If you have run for years and your joints are damaged, swimming offers impact-free exercise.

Swimming provides another huge benefit too. Front crawl and breaststroke allow you to choose when to turn or raise your head to breathe.

Most swimmers breathe with every stroke. There are real benefits to breathing after every few strokes. If you can get into a rhythm, you could leave it for 5 or 6 strokes between each breath. The goal isn't speed, it's consistent exercise and breathing efficiency.

Exercise is beneficial when it improves our muscles, and our respiratory system. Producing lots of CO_2 through movement is the most natural way to improve breathing efficiency at rest. Yoga and cardio exercise such as running or swimming improve fitness, strength and breathing.

Strength Training

Strength is a core part of proper development. While some people tend to focus on one area - upper arms, for example - core strength is key. Core strength is achieved by compound movements. Compound movements require different muscle groups to be active. A squat is an example of a compound exercise.

When we are physically fit, our muscles offer better support to our bones. Exercise improves the body's efficiency in posture and breathing. Humans, before agriculture, caught meat. The process of running-down an animal requires endurance and the ability to sweat lots to stay cool, which many believe is why we are far less hairy than any other ape. The process of moving the hunted animal requires strength. Early humans were relentless endurance athletes.

The core exercises that everyone should do include squats, planks, push ups, lunges and crunches.

Health Quadrant IV: Vitamin D

Vitamin D reduces inflammation in everyone. When it's deficient, inflammation flourishes and the Health Quadrant is severely weakened. When it's abundant, overall health is fortified.

How To Produce Vitamin D - Sunshine

The simplest method to produce Vitamin D is through sunlight hitting our skin. UBV radiation converts to Vitamin D. I recommend people spend 15-30 minutes a day in direct sunlight after 10am and before 4pm. Your lower arms and legs should be exposed.

However, if you are fair skinned and you live at a hotter latitude to your ancestors, you need to be very careful. We evolved to develop the perfect balance of skin protection and Vitamin D absorption. For equatorial Africans, this meant lots of melanin (protection) and extreme sun exposure (powerful sunshine for Vitamin D absorption.) For Scottish people, this meant very little melanin (a low need for protection) and low levels of sunshine (a high need for absorption) which seeped through the tree canopies that covered most of Scotland before humans cleared most of the trees.

White people who live outside their European motherland should be very vigilant about sun exposure. When you have low levels of protection, you are better at absorbing sunshine. Stronger sun in people who evolved to expect smaller amount increases the risks sunburn and skin cancer. Conversely, those who evolved for stronger sunshine, who moved to areas with weaker sunshine are likely to be very deficient in Vitamin D. They are very protected but not efficient at absorbing enough sunshine to meet their Vitamin D requirement. Indeed, most people today spend far more time out of the sunshine than we used to. Most of us are dangerously Vitamin D deficient.

How To Produce Vitamin D - Diet

Changing your diet can improve Vitamin D. Fish live far away from the sun's powerful rays and have evolved to produce Vitamin D internally. For this reason, oily fish contains lots of Vitamin D. Supplementing your diet with sources of Vitamin D is beneficial, if you aren't intolerant to those foods. However, dietary Vitamin D provides far less Vitamin D than sunlight.

The best food sources are salmon, mackerel and sardines. Other foods high in Vitamin D are red meat, liver and egg yolks.

How To Produce Vitamin D - Supplements

Increasing Vitamin D is easy through supplementation. I strongly recommend ordering a Vitamin D test. You will likely find that you are deficient. Supplements are the safest way to produce sufficient Vitamin D.

Here are the ranges of Vitamin D levels In the blood:

Less than 20 ng/ml	Deficient
20-29 ng/ml	Insufficient
30-39 ng/ml	Sufficient
40-59 ng/ml	Safe
60-89 ng/ml	Optimal
Greater than 150 ng/ml	Toxic

To safely reach optimal levels, Vitamin D3 should be taken with Vitamin K2 and Magnesium and Zinc. It's better to start with a high dose than a low dose, as Vitamin D takes a long time to build up in the body.

If you don't get much sunlight, and you don't supplement Vitamin D, order some 10,000 IU Vitamin D tablets. Every 3 months, you should order a new Vitamin D test.

When you have reached between 40 and 89 ng/ml in the blood, you can switch to a maintenance dose. I then recommend 4,000 IU of Vitamin D per day. To protect against possible calcification, which can occur with super-high, consistent doses of 50,000 IU or over per day, I also recommend 400 ug of Vitamin K2, 4mg Zinc and 33 mg Magnesium.

For links to my recommended supplements and Vitamin D tests, visit http://tcarneybowles.com/vitamind. We have created a subscription service so that you can get your required supplements and tests, year-round. This is the final way to strengthen your health Quadrant and retain - or reclaim - your health potential.

Facial Development In History

In our past, children with poor mouth posture were told; *"Your face will stick like that if the wind changes."* This wasn't a myth. It was knowledge from our collective memory as a species that has been forgotten since the Industrial Revolution. Since then, most people have poor mouth posture (and habits.)

The term *"mouth-breather"* is an insult levelled at those who have poor mouth posture and breathing habits. *"Gormless"* is attributed to those with open mouths. *"Slack jaw"* is another derogatory term to describe someone who keeps their mouth hanging open. The term *"knuckle-dragger"* is used to describe individuals with poor body posture. These physical manifestations of lower intelligence are supported by scientific evidence. (See *Beauty Is Contagious – The Theory of Propinquity*.) They also affect facial development.

A few centuries ago, cutlery prompted scorn and derision. For good reason: It would later be proven that use of cutlery degrades jaw alignment. (See *Beauty Quadrant II: How To Eat… (Further Reading)*.) It's only in very recent human history that jaws are not perfectly aligned.

In the 1860s, wisdom tooth extraction became common as society shifted to eating predominantly soft, cooked meals – a drastic, unprecedented change. Our weakened facial musculature led to underdeveloped jaws, leaving less room for all of our teeth. After World War II, food processors meant babies had no need to chew at all. Puréed foods and bottle feeding cause an infantile suckle to remain; stopping the development of a full adult swallow. These are some of the habits that contribute to facial disproportion.

It doesn't begin like this! At birth, babies have virtually identical facial proportions. Physical forces in the womb are virtually identical from one mother to another. Baby features differ, but their proportions do not. Proportions change as we age because the forces on the face after birth are much more diverse and complex than the forces in the womb. A baby's cuteness is retained or lost as their face develops. It takes the outside world, and unnatural forces, for disproportion to form.

Human faces grow far more outside the womb than other animal, and our comparatively underdeveloped faces rely on environmental forces to fully shape them. (See *Why Do All Babies Have Similar Facial Proportions?*)

I coin the term *beauty potential*. All of us are born with the potential to be beautiful. Environmental forces snatch that potential away from most of us in the first 15 years of life. When we retain our genetic potentials, rather than succumbing to our vulnerabilities, we hold on to our innate beauty potential. Just as we have plasticity in our muscles and heights, our brains and immune systems, we have *facial plasticity* too.

Beauty is not attained: It's retained, or it's lost.

What Caused This Book To Be Written...

I booked a dentist in Harley Street, London, to make a stray tooth inline with the others. She asked for pictures before I arrived. Email sent, I met her in a beautiful old building up three flights of creaky stairs. As I sat down, she told me, almost apologetically, that I have a recessed upper jaw (maxilla). She couldn't make my tooth bigger because I have a cross bite, meaning one of my lower teeth would crash into the extension of the upper tooth when I ate or spoke or slept.

She put me in touch with an orthodontist. He said I had a crossbite, a recessed maxilla, an underbite and that I'd require jaw surgery.

No-one had told me my face was deficient before. Although, immediately, I knew it was true. I discovered this at 32 years of age. Three dentists had seen that one of my upper jaw teeth was missing. One told me I had an underbite. Yet, I'd never heard about recessed maxillae. I knew I wasn't beautiful. I knew that some people were very good looking and I wasn't among them. And now I knew why.

At home, I read and researched. I learned that my habits and lifestyle after my birth caused the deficiencies in my face. I learned how deficiencies form. I also compared modern levels of jaw deficiency with archaeological evidence going back to the Stone Age. Crooked teeth and jaw misalignment were almost non-existent in our Stone Age ancestors. Could environmental factors really cause faces to change so dramatically? I had an appointment with one of London's best private jaw surgeons, and I wanted to find out.

When we met, he confirmed that I was a perfect candidate for surgery. I had a long face, a recessed maxilla, an underbite and a crossbite. He said that it developed from childhood. I cut in, "Because of mouth breathing?"

"Yes, exactly," He continued, "The body changes growth patterns based on how you hold your face."

"Epigenetics?"

"Yes, exactly epigenetics. It's fair to say that if you hadn't held your mouth open, you wouldn't be seeing me now."

I was stunned. A highly respected cranio-facial surgeon confirmed that faces are shaped, sometimes dramatically, by how we live. He went on to describe that patients who breathe wrongly, swallow wrongly, and who's resting mouth posture is wrong are always the ones who require this kind of surgery. Those who didn't use their jaws to chew saw facial decline. He said bottle-feeding and pacifiers were, "Good for keeping a baby quiet, but terrible for the development of their jaws."

Bad habits cause facial deformity. Adult beauty is not an innate, genetic lottery. It's shaped by how we use our faces. He knew it. But until that trip, I didn't. Most people don't, and that struck me as crazy. I was angry that most of society didn't know this. Facial beauty isn't predetermined by our genes. The truth is far more complicated and nuanced. We are shaped by our habits, lifestyles, and vulnerabilities to chronic inflammation. If you had a blocked nose when you were 4 years old due to hay fever (as I did) you will develop a habit of mouth breathing (as I did). This causes facial proportions and beauty potential to slip away.

He told me that snoring (which I did) and sleep apnea are a byproduct of jaw recession, as the airway becomes too small. And that in our distant past, people were likely "far better looking" as they didn't encounter these issues.

It's popular these days to advise people to grow to love their imperfections. That certainly has its place in society and it's necessary to our collective emotional wellbeing. A book about making peace with imperfections would be psychological in nature. This book is not psychologically-based and it doesn't aim or intend to be. This is a physiological book, solely focused on optimising beauty and health, as they go hand-on-hand. From now on, emotions regarding loss of beauty potential have no place in this book. Why beauty potential is lost, and how to mitigate against it is my sole aim.

The Skull Record Reveals Ugliness Is A Disease of Civilisation

Anthropologist and curator of the Morton Collection of about 1,000 skulls, Janet Monge, was asked by the *New York Times Magazine* if she had ever seen an ancient skull with crooked teeth or misaligned jaws. Her response was emphatic: *"No, not one. Ever."*[1] All the skulls in her collection have *"perfect"* bites, with jaws that met beautifully. She told WHYY-FM: **"Nobody in the past had dental problems**... *nobody... It's like the upper jaw - the maxilla - and lower jaw - the mandible - are...* **perfectly in unity** *with each other and the interesting thing is that was* **everybody in human history.**"[2] [My emphasis.] Monge showed the interviewer a 5,000 year old skull from Iran, who recounts, *"it had a Hollywood smile. Straight, white, symmetrical."* This was normal. This was everyone.

Malocclusion and improper facial development are seen by looking at the teeth and jaws. A skull stripped to tooth and bone reveals improper development, as teeth may be crooked or impacted, and jaws misaligned. Impacted wisdom teeth are particularly revealing because they show that the mouth didn't grow *forwards* enough. Clark Spencer Larsen noted that 10,000 years ago everyone grew healthy, non-impacted wisdom teeth.[3] All mouths grew forwards before the agricultural revolution, leaving plenty of space for all of their teeth.

Forward growth is caused by natural mouth posture, eating as our ancestors ate, and adult swallowing. That represents three tenets of the Beauty Quadrant. These days, most wisdom teeth are impacted or they don't erupt, most people's mouths are too small and their jaws are recessed.

Richard Klein, a Stanford evolutionist with expert knowledge of our species' fossil record, revealed that he had *never* seen malocclusion (jaw misalignment) in an early human skull.[4] Evolutionary biologist, Daniel Lieberman, states in his book, *The Story of the Human Body*:

> *The museum I work in has thousands of ancient skulls from all over the world. Most of the skulls from the last few hundred years are a dentist's nightmare: they are filled with cavities and infections, the teeth are crowded into the jaw, and about one-quarter of them have impacted teeth. The skulls of preindustrial farmers are also riddled with cavities and painful-looking abscesses, but less than 5 percent of them have impacted wisdom teeth. In contrast, most of the hunter-gatherers had nearly perfect dental health. Apparently, orthodontists and dentists were rarely necessary in the Stone Age.*[5]

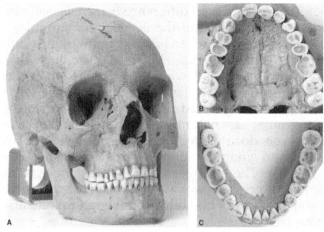

Figure 35 – Norwegian skull with natural occlusion and room for all teeth. (Photos courtesy of American Journal of Orthodontics and Dento-facial Orthopedics)

Figure 35 is the skull of a man from the 14th century in Oslo, Norway. You'll notice that the molar teeth are worn flat. That's because of the sheer amount of chewing hard food that was required to be well-nourished. His teeth are aligned, upper and lower jaws meet perfectly and there are no crooked or missing teeth. His jaws are forward grown and his cheekbones project outwards.

Figure 36 – The Begg skull. (Image courtesy of John Mew.)

Figure 36 is a traditional skull from Australia. His teeth are straight and aligned, including his wisdom teeth, which have erupted as nature intended. PR Begg, who studied this skull, was moved to say malocclusion is *"a disease of modern civilisation."*[6] I believe it goes further. Lost beauty potential, through facial disproportion, is also a disease of modern civilisation. Malocclusion is simply a symptom of development gone wrong.

Weston Price photographed many different groups of people in the early 20th Century. Intriguingly, he went to 14 different countries and saw a stark but very consistent difference *in every instance* between the industrialised communities and the isolated communities from each country he visited, at a time when isolated communities still existed in most countries. Without fail, those in isolated groups - who lived pre-industrialised lifestyles - had wider jaws, more proportional faces, healthier teeth and better jaw alignment. The genes in the industrialised groups expressed themselves worse than the genes in the isolated groups, as natural environmental expectations were unmet. Price even documented the difference in facial proportion between older and younger siblings when they shifted to a more industrial lifestyle. The younger child had a longer, slimmer face, crooked teeth and recessed jaws, where his older brother did not. The older sibling spent more of his childhood living pre-industrially, and it showed on his face.

John Mew - the father of orthotropics, which focuses on growing jaws forwards - took an average of 1,500 modern Swedish soldiers jaws, then overlaid the average onto Begg's skull by way of comparing how different modern faces are. (See *Figure 11, page 16.*) The overlay shows that modern life has led to the vertical elongation and flattening of our faces. The difference is stark. The modern overlay is an average of healthy, fit Swedish soldiers, not society's worst cases. It's a reflection of members of society healthy enough to pass tests to serve in the military. Seeing a recessed face overlaid on that skull would be starker still.

The biggest facial changes between generations are caused by environmental, not genetic forces.

Most skulls from before the 1780s have excellent alignment. Every example from 12,000 years ago and before was beautifully formed. Only modern skulls from westernised societies have disproportion. The skulls above aren't cherry-picked. They were common, normal and natural - *representing everybody in human history.*

All Stone Age skulls have beautiful wide, forward-projected upper and lower jaws - the key elements of beauty. This proportional growth occurs when environmental expectations - found in the Beauty Quadrant - are realised. Virtually every hunter-gatherer achieved ideal growth; forward grown jaws, wide and short faces, and perfectly aligned, straight teeth with bites that fit in perfect unity. They naturally adhered to the Beauty & Health Quadrants. We still have the Stone Age DNA of our ancestors, but we grow up in *vastly* different environments. I can't stress this enough; working in an office and snacking on Coke and donuts has nothing in common with hunting wilderbeast in the plains of Africa. Or with catching deer in European forests. The damage to our Health Quadrant often causes our Beauty Quadrant to be heavily compromised.

This doesn't mean that we have to live naked in the forests and plains! All we have to do, to benefit as they did, is apply the Quadrants to match the environmental forces that shape beauty and health.

Intergenerational Changes

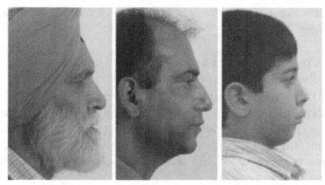

Figure 37 – Three generations of facial decline after a grandfather (left) moved to England as a young man. His son (centre) has recessed jaws. His grandson (right) has even more jaw recession. (Images courtesy of John Mew.)

Changes in how we live cause changes in facial development. This is seen intergenerationally and, indeed, intragenerationally. (See *Figure 37*.) Intergenerational changes have been witnessed in many different groups, by Weston Price and by researchers looking at the Inuits.

They are also seen when families emigrate to Westernised societies. Typically the first generation retain facial proportion. The second generation, born in western society, eat their parents food at home and western food at school. By the third generation, western lifestyles have fully taken hold and their faces suffer from recession. While a few children can maintain the Beauty Quadrant in Western societies, most can't.

When Inuit populations became Canadian citizens, they were given food stamps and social housing. Some would argue that this was progress. However, in terms of health and facial development, it was as though a plague had descended on their young. L. M. Waugh documented, in 1937, that the Inuit people suffered in a single generation.[7] Parents who grew up on the ice gave birth to children who grew up in social housing. These children were fed cheap, mass-produced, food-stamp diets. They developed tooth and jaw issues that their ancestors had never contended with. They were the first generation in their people's history to encounter these problems *en masse*. This wasn't a genetic issue. It was an environmental issue. The children had strayed too far from the developmental benefits of natural living. Their environmental expectations were suddenly and drastically unmet.

In 1971, BF Wood studied another Inuit population. He noted that the increase in cavities, crooked teeth and jaw misalignment, *"has been shown to be caused by the change from a primitive diet of meat and fat to one which incorporates the starches and refined sugars introduced by the white man."*[8]

A British study, which looked at Chinese families who emigrated, found that the children - exposed to a Western diet and lifestyle - had more dental issues than their parents who grew up in China.[9] The study posits that mouth posture, chronic allergies (including respiratory inflammation) and a soft diet were the causes of this shift, and neatly suggests that 'urban migration' is the catalyst to the observed changes. New environments caused the shift in facial development in a single generation.

X-rays of modern people with malocclusion are startling when compared with ancient skulls. The ancient skulls differ from each other slightly. Modern people's skulls can differ astronomically. Now we see overbites, underbites, both jaws being recessed, crossbites, and openbites, where upper and lower teeth don't touch when the mouth is closed. There is virtually no record of malocclusion in ancient skulls and there are very few with perfect occlusion in modern skulls.

Intragenerational Changes

Changes in one individual give a compelling case for environments changing facial structure. Take the boy who was gifted a gerbil that lived in his bedroom. (See *Figure 38, overleaf.*) At age 10, his facial structure was excellent. By age 17, his beauty and health potentials had dramatically declined. We can see this decline in his disproportional facial development. In this case his genes were expressing themselves excellently, before a huge, sudden shift stripped his potentials and exposed his vulnerabilities. What on earth happened?

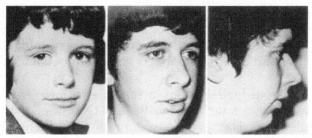

Figure 38 – A 10-year old boy (right) with good facial development, which was compromised by poor mouth posture caused by allergies. Age 17 (center & right), his face has grown downwards and he doesn't maintain natural mouth posture. (Images courtesy of John Mew.)

His face was well-developed, aged 10. Then negative environmental pressures turned "good genetics" into "bad genetics." The gerbil caused an allergic reaction which damaged his breathing. With a blocked nose, his mouth posture was destroyed. He slept with a blocked nose, his mouth was open, his jaws became recessed, his under-eye support fell away. The damage to his *Health Quadrant* affected his *Beauty Quadrant*. The result was a far less proportional face.

All young children are beautiful. Their beauty potential can slip away in many unexpected ways, like a gerbil sharing a child's bedroom. The boys potentials turned to vulnerabilities.

We believe what we see. We have no collective memory of how we developed before industrialisation or agriculture. We believe that the faces we see are perfectly natural. They are not. We believe, erroneously, that people who would have developed disproportionally in our ancient past would have died young. Yet, there is no evidence of disproportion occurring in the skeletons of our distant ancestors.

A Unified Framework for Facial Beauty

Most people who have written about the facial changes they witnessed believe that one cause - one part of one Quadrant - adversely affected facial development. Charles Darwin suggested that how you eat - soft cooked food versus harder uncooked food - made jaws shorter and more recessed. Weston Price felt that what you eat causes physical degeneration through lack of nutrients. John Mew talks about nearly every aspect of the Beauty Quadrant, except for one aspect of how we eat.

We are left with space for a unified framework for beauty that will work for every child. The Beauty and Health Quadrants aim to fill his hole. This book is about maximising our *Beauty & Health Quadrants* so that our beauty and health potentials can be retained and realised.

This book is front-loaded with actionable principles that you've already read. First we tackled the Beauty Quadrant, which directly affects facial beauty. Then we focused on the Health Quadrant, which indirectly affects the Beauty Quadrant and directly affects lifelong health. The *why we grow this way,* for those interested, occurs from here.

The Beauty & The Health Quadrants: Environmental Forces That Shape The Face

The Blueprint

Imagine a perfect house blueprint. Two houses have the exact same blueprint. House One is built on solid granite and House Two is built on unstable soil. House One uses strong mortar. House Two uses weak mortar that decays and rots over time. The genetic blueprint of both houses is the same. You can put all the bricks in the same place. You can have the same size windows. Yet, when you go back later, the house with weak foundations and weak mortar might be wonky, sinking, falling apart and asymmetrical. There might be a crack in one of the walls. The floors might be uneven. Same design, same blueprint, different outcome.

The human face has a perfect blueprint. What separates a perfectly formed face from an imperfectly formed face is the forces acting on it, just like with the two houses above. If the Beauty Quadrant and Health Quadrant are corrupted, facial foundations are weak, and facial growth is compromised, ideal facial development is lost.

How Beauty Is Retained...

The *Beauty Quadrant* represents the four natural facial forces that directly shape the face; mouth posture, how we eat, swallowing and body posture. These environmental expectations are *necessary* for ideal facial proportions and symmetry. Apply them optimally and beauty flourishes. When these essential forces aren't applied, beauty potential slips away.

A growing face requires the forces of natural mouth posture (where the mouth is closed and nose breathing is a natural byproduct), eating and breaking down tough foods (so that strong jaws develop), a natural adult swallow (prompted by breast feeding then swallowing tough, non-puréed foods), and upright body posture. Disrupting these natural, expected facial forces causes unnatural facial development.

It's well established, for example, that prolonged pacifier use causes jaw misalignment and crooked teeth. The unnatural force - the pacifier - disrupts natural mouth posture and reshapes teeth and jaws.

Unnatural forces include having an open mouth (or filling a mouth with unnatural objects), eating soft foods and not chewing enough, not developing an adult swallow, and poor head and body alignment.

The Health Quadrant - breathing, what we eat and when, exercise and Vitamin D - acts indirectly. It either supports our ability to maintain Beauty Quadrant forces, or it acts as a great disruptor. Mouth breathing, for example, corrupts the first element of both quadrants; mouth posture and breathing. It's often caused by, and exacerbates, chronic inflammation. No chronic inflammation means the nose is clear of mucus, so the mouth can be closed (correcting mouth posture and breathing) and beauty potential is more easily retained. The Health Quadrant lets us live free from chronic inflammation so that the Beauty Quadrant can be maintained.

Modern life has corrupted both Quadrants. This corruption affects facial development and our long term health. When we apply *Beauty* and *Health Quadrants* to their full virtuous potential, beautiful and healthy people emerge. When they are corrupted the after-effects are seen, resulting in facial disproportion and lifelong poor heath. Just as we have beauty potential, we have health potential. Combined, they represent our genetic potential. We need to maintain both Quadrants to achieve our maximum potentials.

Unnatural Pressures Cause Unnatural Growth

Unnatural environmental pressures can change the way we grow and develop. *Spaceflight* osteopenia is a condition faced by astronauts, who lose between 1-2% of their bone mass per month in zero-gravity. Zero gravity is such a drastic environmental change of force on bones that an astronaut's DNA's bone-regulation blueprint is transformed in space. This is epigenetics in action. Epigenetic changes occur when an environmental trigger switches the way genes express. For astronauts, the trigger of zero gravity causes bone size-regulating genes to reduce bone mass. It leads to a predictable and consistent loss of bone mass, faced by every astronaut who has spent time in space. The *environmental expectation* of gravity is not met, so astronaut bones shrink.

Back on earth, failure to meet the environmental expectations that shape faces changes how they grow. It leads to disproportion and, often, worse health. Height is a well-understood similar example. Height changed dramatically when the agricultural revolution took hold. The average height before agriculture was 5'10" for men and 5'6" for women. The switch to less-varied, grain-heavy diets was a nutritional disaster. Men became 5'5" on average, and women 5'1". The vulnerability to height-loss was triggered only when the nutritional content of our diets was impaired by agriculture.

In a similar way, certain triggers in modern life change the growth of our faces when facial environmental expectations are unmet. These triggers, when the expected forces, habits and lifestyles of our stone age ancestors are not applied, lead to lost beauty potential. Our faces change proportions - to our detriment - when environmental expectations are unmet. Some modern environmental pressures are as strange to our faces as zero gravity is to our bones.

*Unmet environmental expectations consistently corrupt
facial development.*

Each Beauty Quadrant and Health Quadrant tenet should be viewed as a dial, not a switch. We can maximise each dial in two ways. First is how close to optimal you are - the *degree*. Second is the amount of time you maintain the optimal degree - the *duration*. For all the tenets, we should aim for optimal degree and duration.

The *Beauty & Health Quadrants* are Nature's Laws. They are Nature's expected forces that guide healthy facial development. For most of human history, as we lived as hunter gatherers, these laws were naturally applied because of how we lived.

As we delve deeper into this book, the impacts of these eight environmental expectations on facial development will become clear. All the tenets are environmental; meaning all can be changed and maximised by taking action. Our ability to change these facial forces means we can shape our beauty and our health.

We don't - and can't - grow in isolation from our environments. These environmental expectations, when met, cause our teeth - which erupt in more-or-less the right places - to end up in exactly the right positions. The forces acting on the mouth nudge teeth and jaws into optimal alignment. The passive force of natural mouth posture hold teeth and jaws in their correct place at rest; through the tongue, lips, cheeks and jaw muscles. Active forces of swallowing, tearing, biting and chewing cause jaws to be pulled forwards and teeth to be perfectly aligned when in motion. When these expected forces are unmet, the whole body becomes more susceptible to vulnerabilities in place of potentials.

Beauty Quadrant I: Mouth Posture (Further Reading)

Native Americans Versus Industrialised Americans

In 1797, Julian Ursyn Niemcewicz first visited the United States of America from Europe and saw Native Americans and their *"beautiful teeth"*.[1] Crooked teeth are caused by improperly developed jaws, which form disproportional faces. Yet, while Niemcewicz focused on teeth, George Catlin looked more broadly at differences between contemporary "civilised" society and native communities in the 1830s.

Catlin - explorer, portrait artist and lawyer - spent those years, *"observing the healthy condition and **physical perfection** of those [native] people... contrasted with... **deformities**, in civilized communities"*. [My emphasis.] After seeing such well-developed Native American faces, he witnessed in civilised society, *"a derangement and deformity of the teeth, and disfigurement of the mouth and the whole face, which are not natural."*[2]

Native Americans adhered to nature's expectations, giving them, *"beauty and symmetry"*.[3] He saw that beautiful Western people occasionally emerge. Yet, Native Americans showed, *"a greater average of good looks, than an equal community of any Civilized people."*[4]

Catlin grew up in the industrialised east of the USA where facial disproportion and crooked teeth were common. The differences he saw compelled him to write the book, *Shut Your Mouth and Save Your Life*. He believed that mouth posture and breathing were the reason Native Americans reached their genetic potentials, while unnatural mouth posture and mouth-breathing exposed industrialised people to their genetic vulnerabilities.

Native Americans Knew Mouth Posture Shapes Faces

When confronted by unnatural western mouth posture, Native Americans were so shocked that they called whites, *"black mouths,"* in *"disgust with the expression of open and black mouths."*[5] To them, open mouths and mouth breathing provoked revulsion. This wasn't just reflected in their response to white people. When their own children dared to hang their mouths open, Native American mothers were quick to act:

> *The Savage infant... breathing the natural and wholesome air, generally from instinct, closes its mouth during its sleep; and in all cases of exception the mother rigidly (and cruelly, if necessary) enforces Nature's Law in the manner explained, until the habit is fixed for life, of the importance of which she seems to be perfectly well aware.*[6]

Mothers willing to go to cruel lengths to enforce natural mouth posture and breathing shows its importance. Having contrasted what he saw in Native Americans and contemporary American society, Catlin concluded that the habit changes the face, facial structure doesn't cause the habit.

> *No man or woman with a handsome set of teeth keeps the mouth habitually open; and every person with an unnatural derangement of the teeth is as sure seldom to have it shut. This is not because the derangement of the teeth has made the habit, but because the habit has caused the derangement of the teeth.*[7]

John Mew & Orthotropics

John Mew, who created the Orthotropic method of facial growth and dental occlusion, understands how to unlock beauty potential. Three and a half of the four tenets in the Beauty Quadrant are highlighted by Mew. He believes that mouth posture, swallowing, chewing tough foods and body posture all impact facial proportion and symmetry. (Only missing clamping and tearing food with hands and jaws.) Mew estimates that 98% of people have incorrect mouth posture and therefore 98% of people have some form of facial deformity. The other 2% are the exceptionally good-looking. Natural mouth posture is the single most important requiremet to retain good looks.

The Ominous Literature on Open Mouths

Scientists have compared mouth breathers to nose breathers and found that their faces develop differently. Natural resting mouth posture is impossible for mouth breathers, and open mouth posture is the cause of negative facial changes. The findings are chilling for those who want to retain beauty potential.

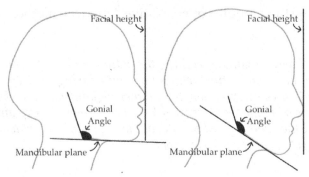

Figure 39 – Ideal faces have a short facial height, low gonial angle and a low mandibular plane (left). Poorly proportioned faces have the opposite (right).

Mouth breathing and unnatural mouth posture cause, *"increased facial height, mandibular plane angle and gonial angle."*[8] (See *Figure 39.*) Jaws become recessed and narrower: *"mouth breathers had longer faces with narrower maxillae and retrognathic jaws."*[9] This looks worse, leaves less room for the nasal cavity in both forwards and lateral dimensions, less room for teeth in the jaws, and causes less attractive faces. It also changes soft tissue, making the lips appear thinner and smaller, and the cheeks less hollow.

When the facial bones drop and rotate downwards - which always happens when natural mouth posture is not applied - you have less under-eye support; more chance of scleral show; droopy eyes; flatter and narrower cheekbones, maxilla and mandible; and a narrower face, because the facial bones take less forwards space and instead descend. *"Mouth breathers demonstrated considerable backward and downward rotation of the mandible, increased overjet... a higher palatal plane, and narrowing of both upper and lower arches"*[10]

Scientists recognise that poor mouth posture is the issue: *"open mouth posture, low posture of the tongue... [and] mouth-breathing at night, were associated with skeletal features expressing an increased open vertical configuration and mandibular retrognathism."*[11] Mouth breathing at night is why mouth tape is necessary.

Mouth posture is the biggest differentiator for facial development. This is a scientific proof that the general public has no idea about, and that needs to change.

Disproportion makes you look and feel worse - destroying beauty and health potentials. When the Laws of Natural Mouth Posture are ignored or misapplied, it's to the detriment of beauty and health.

A study in China looked at tongue pressure against the palate in people with naturally straight teeth and jaws. They only found 19 who qualified, out of the 189 candidates who all thought they had no need for orthodontics. Most of the excluded candidates had crooked teeth and jaw misalignment. The 19 who were selected had no malocclusion and no history of, or need for, orthodontics. All 19 applied tongue pressure to the hard palate consistently.[12] The study also found that participants with a longer duration swallow had a longer palate arch depth – which translates to more forward growth.

The single most important thing children can do for their beauty potential is to *always* apply natural mouth posture.

Mouth Posture & Me

As a child I mouth-breathed constantly, because my nose was often blocked, then the open-mouthed habit formed. (It is no coincidence that the first Beauty Quadrant tenet and the first Health Quadrant tenet - mouth posture and breathing - support or disrupt each other.) I was often told by grown-ups in the late 1980s and early 1990s, "If the wind changes you face will stick like that." I tested the hypothesis, stood outside until the wind shifted direction, and felt that I had completely disproved the hypothesis. My face was exactly the same as before!

The reality, over a long enough timeline, is exactly the opposite of my naive test. Unfortunately, I, like most children, took what the adults said literally. What I should have been told was, "If you keep that improper mouth posture, your face will slowly become ugly, and you will become sick." After which, I should have been taught the laws of natural mouth posture.

Beauty Quadrant II: How To Eat... (Further Reading)

We never consider "how to eat" beyond what we are taught. Children eat, and get a lifelong taste for, what their parents feed them. The potentials and vulnerabilities which affected your parents and grandparents will be the same potentials and vulnerabilities which affect you, given that your environments mirror theirs (unless in the last few generations your family has emigrated to a more western society.) If you see two expectant parents with recessed jaws, their child is very likely to form recessed jaws too. This is an environmental manifestation. Dad mouth-breathes? Mum eats soft foods like pizza and ice cream? Parents are inflamed by their diet? Baby will likely follow on all counts.

Forks & Chopsticks Corrupted Our Faces

Before researching this book, I'd have never believed that something as simple as a fork or chopsticks could shape our faces. Yet, it's a fact.

Knives, forks and chopsticks compromise forward growth and jaw alignment.

Dentists seek an overbite when they force tooth movement with braces. The overhang of our upper teeth over our lower teeth is supposed to be the "correct" position for our teeth. Yet, the overbite is so recent that it was seen nowhere in the skull record of the Western world beyond about 1780. Before then, everyone had an edge-to-edge bite. This fact troubled Charles Loring Brace IV, an anthropologist obsessed with the modern emergence the overbites, which sprung seemingly without rhyme or reason. His hunch that fork-use caused overbites lingered as just that - a hunch - for three long decades.

He looked at Western European skulls first and sure enough, overbites emerged as forks became widespread. Cutlery-use in America, crucially, spread a few decades *later* than in Europe. Brace hoped to see if the shift in overbites in America coincided with the shift in the use of forks. Finding quality skull samples from that narrow window in the early 19th Century proved difficult. Yet, eventually, his search bore fruit.

In Rochester, New York, bodies from a prison, an insane asylum, and a workhouse, buried in an unmarked cemetery, gave Brace solid evidence. Of the fifteen bodies, during the transition to cutlery use in America, ten bodies had an edge-to-edge bite. A slither of proof. When forks were used less in America, overbites were significantly less common.

China confirmed his hypothesis. Chinese meals have been chopped into bite-sized, chopstick-friendly chunks since way back in the Song dynasty (960-1279 AD). The first movers with this new table technology were the aristocracy. Soon, chopsticks made their way into the homes of ordinary Chinese families.

Brace found, in the Shanghai Natural History Museum, the absolute proof to his hypothesis. A graduate student - alive during the Song dynasty and pickled in vat ever since - had, Brace observed, *"the deep overbite of the modern Chinese!"*[1]

Brace discovered that the Chinese overbite was 800 - 1,000 years older than the European overbite. As he analysed more Chinese teeth, he found that most Chinese had overbites. The exception was some peasants who, well into the 20th Century, had edge-to-edge bites. These poorest-of-the-poor still used their hands to eat.

What makes forks and chopsticks transform our faces?

The size of the food we eat plays a role in our physiology. The way we transfer food from plate to mouth, how much we transfer, and how we break it up when it gets there all play a role in our bites. Tearing food apart between clamped jaws with hands nudges the jaws forwards with every single bite. Under these forces, the cranial sutures on the palate are pulled apart, and new bone forms as we grow into adulthood. This is an environmental expectation that virtually none of us fulfil. Without it, the lower jaw sits behind the upper jaw, so the edge-to-edge bite no longer occurs. Indeed, in modern humans, both jaws are generally more recessed than they should, without the clamping and tearing action that eating with hands requires. The very act of cutting food into little pieces before it reaches the mouth changed faces forever.

The very sudden shift of the lower jaw sitting further back than the upper jaw was driven by the very sudden shift to cutlery. As the knives we used to cut became blunter and morsels became smaller and softer, the amount we needed to chew plummeted. Since cutlery use, there is no biting force that applies outward force to the upper and lower jaws.

Forks Weren't Always Fashionable

We may think using hands to eat is rude and unsightly. Forks were once viewed in the same way. A Byzantine princess in the 11th Century was damned by St. Peter Damian for her "excessive delicacy". In 1605, French satirist Thomas Artus wrote that fork-use was obscene. He viewed Henri II and his courtiers with derision because they "never touch meat with their hands but with forks".

The only nation who used forks before the 17th Century was Italy. Pasta required the deftness of the fork to eat it comfortably. British sailors rejected forks for being effeminate, in 1897! The collective memory of cutlery being subversive hasn't survived. But being so weak and delicate that you can't tear meat with teeth and hands was clearly looked down upon.

Forks are not a constant in history. They are an accessory that became popular. Today, we wrongly believe they are necessary to the detriment of our beauty potential.

Modern Foods Are Not as Good as We Think

Most fruits and vegetables today are descendants of other plants which were smaller, tougher, harder to break down and less sweet. We would eat roots and seeds and bugs and weeds - often raw. The one constant across every diet and generation was meat. When the seasons changed and edible flora was scarce, we could always rely on meat. The fauna that our distant ancestors ate is far more similar today than the flora they ate.

Julius Caesar landed in Britain and observed:

> *"Most of the inland inhabitants do not sow corn, but live on milk and flesh."*[2]

The Romans were a far more advanced civilisation than the British. However, the Roman nose occurs because of their diet and lifestyle. Introducing grains and potential chronic inflammation causes faces to grow down, giving a lack of support for the nose.

Jaw "Shortening" From Soft, Cooked Food

In 1868, German anthropologist Hermann Schaaffhausen noted of *"civilised"* men, *"the posterior dental portion of the jaw [is] always shortened"*.[3] That's to say, when the wisdom teeth emerged, there was no room for them. Charles Darwin corresponded with Charles Loring Brace (the great-grandfather of the aforementioned Charles Loring Brace IV) in America and Paolo Mantegazza in Italy who all witnessed this shortening, resulting in wisdom teeth needing to be removed. Darwin said, "I am informed by Mr. Brace that it is becoming quite a common practice in the United States to remove some of the molar teeth of children, as the jaw does not grow large enough for the perfect development of the normal number." In four places, Britain, Germany, Italy and the United States, jaws were growing to have less space for teeth in the 19th Century.

These changes occurred in different regions - and different gene pools - at the same time. Crucially, the changes only occurred in "civilised" societies, as they shifted to eating mainly cooked food. Only white people were affected back then, because only white people ate predominantly cooked meals. Other races didn't suffer wisdom tooth problems because their facial forces underwent less change. Today, every race is affected by malocclusion and impacted wisdom teeth, because every race now eats softer, cooked food.

Darwin, the father of the theory of evolution, suggested, *"this shortening may, I presume, be attributed to civilised men habitually feeding on soft, cooked food, and thus using their jaws less."*[4] The man who himself discovered evolutionary genetics put these changes down to environmental forces and not mutations in our genes. Weakened facial musculature has direct negative facial consequences. The lifestyle shift to constant cooking also caused an indirect threat. Soft, cooked foods (and low levels of Vitamin D in industrialised societies) increase the chance of inflammation. Inflammation often leads to mouth breathing, limiting the development of a full adult swallow, and body posture declines. Both the Beauty Quadrant and the Health Quadrant are impacted.

Human Clinical Studies on Bite Force & Facial Structure

There is a strong correlation between maximum bite force and the following facial dimensions; lower facial height, lower jaw width, and forward facial growth.[5] People with stronger maximum bites are more likely to have short, wide, forward-grown faces. Darwin's observations that soft, cooked food caused jaw recession in the 19th Century becomes even more striking when science suggests strong facial muscles correlate with well-developed faces.

Baby faces have very similar proportions and very similar muscle strength, and only environmental forces cause huge deviation that can be observed in later life. Studies have found that people with weak facial musculature have more varied facial structure than those with strong facial musculature. All these variations are variations away from ideal proportions. Furthermore, findings suggest that *"the form of the face partly depends on the strength of the muscles."*[6] People *"with a strong bite force present a well-developed masticatory musculature, smaller anterior facial height (short face)".*[7] Short faces with natural mouth posture and strong muscles can only grow forwards and laterally. People *"with smaller bite force value exhibit a longer anterior and shorter posterior facial height (long face)".*[8] Long faces grow downwards. They are narrower and flatter.

Asymmetry & Chewing

Babies often emerge from the womb with asymmetry, as their bones are incredibly soft, and the birth canal is a tight squeeze! However, this corrects itself in almost all cases. Long-term asymmetry develops for lots of reasons; a lack of space in the mouth; mouth breathing; unnatural mouth posture; when food is chewed on one side of the mouth only; or, when a wisdom tooth doesn't erupt on one side. Often people chew with a one-side bias. This causes asymmetry.[9]

The Danger of Juicing

Calories should be eaten, not blended and drank. Juices don't introduce clamping/biting, tearing or chewing. Considering it also stops the development of an adult swallow (more on this shortly), juices offer nothing positive compared to breaking down food with your jaws. It's far better to grab food like a caveman and eat fruit and vegetables in their natural, raw, uncut state.

The more calories a child consumes as liquid, the more at risk they are of losing beauty and health potentials, even if their smoothies are deemed healthy, green and rich in "super-foods". Long term facial recession often leads to a host of health issues, cold-pressed super-food smoothies be damned.

How To Eat & Me

When I was a boy, I was brought up as a vegetarian, always eating very soft foods. I once joked at a Christmas meal that it required no chewing at all. *Look!* I said as I swallowed a forkful of food without chewing once. We laughed; the implications of active mouth forces being lost on us all.

When my father convinced me to eat meat, I took a bite of tough barbecue lamb. I struggled with all the chewing. It felt endless. My jaws were burning. I spat it out and stuck to vegetables for the rest of the meal! In reality, for the benefit of my face, I should have selected tough meats at every opportunity and slowly chewed them until they were ready to swallow.

Beauty Quadrant III: Swallowing (Further Reading)

Atypical Swallowing

The eruption of teeth signifies the period of transition from an infantile swallow to an adult swallow. Without this successful transition, atypical swallowing takes place.

In an atypical swallow the tip of the tongue touches the teeth. Sometimes the tongue rests between the teeth during swallowing, which leads to an open bite in the front teeth. Always, no matter how you swallow atypically, the tongue is lower in the mouth than it is during a natural adult swallow. The main reasons that atypical swallowing remains include; cutlery use during feeding, mouth breathing, thumb sucking, and pacifier use.

When you force-feed a baby, by putting food on a spoon and putting it in a baby's mouth, babies don't wait until this alien object - the spoon - is removed from the mouth before they swallow. The tongue can't press firmly against the palate to swallow, as a spoon is placed between tongue and palate, so babies find other ways to swallow their food.

When we mouth breathe, the tongue must drop in the mouth for breathing to occur. When a child has a fully blocked nose, they don't swallow with strong tongue pressure against the roof of the mouth, because they are breathing through their mouth.

Thumb sucking and pacifier use inhibit natural adult swallowing in the same way that spoons in the mouth do. The path of the tongue to the palate is impeded. Children suckle saliva down instead of pressing the tongue against the palate. This impedes natural swallowing.

All these events cause compensations. Instead of developing a full adult swallow, babies compensate by developing less optimal ways to swallow. When that habit sticks, the face grows disproportionally. There is a strong link between malocclusion and atypical swallowing. The defining causes of this are; the tongue, the upper and lower teeth touching, and the lips, just as with natural mouth posture.

The Great Force - Your Tongue

When dentists apply indicator paste we know that those with less paste remaining on their palate tend to have better facial proportions, straighter teeth, wider dental arches, higher cheekbones, more forward growth, a lower instance of breathing issues and more beauty, as the tongue shifts the paste.

For people with a poor swallow, the tongue doesn't apply proper pressure in the right place. Instead of taking its natural, dominant role in swallowing, it allows the lips and the cheeks to join in. In this scenario, the tongue avoids the palate and doesn't create strong suction against it. As mouth posture shows and swallowing confirms, a palate-avoidant tongue loses genetic potentials.

A tongue wrecks beauty potential when it avoids the palate during a swallow, sucks on the teeth to generate suction, or it goes between the upper and lower teeth in a tongue-thrust. The forces for a weak swallow come from lips and overactive cheeks, as much as the tongue. The lips are often active, the upper and lower teeth don't touch, and the muscles around the mouth, rather than the tongue in the mouth, force an atypical swallow.

The tongue is the great force of beauty, at rest and in action. In the Beauty Quadrant, the tongue plays a central role in all three of the face-focused tenets - natural mouth posture, swallowing, and how you eat. The tongue must be high against the palate as often as possible. It's the maxilla's strongest support structure. That force - the tongue, working alone, against the palate - is how natural, adult swallowing occurs.

Facial Force Differences Between A Natural Adult Swallow & An Atypical Swallow

In a natural adult swallow, the tongue pushes strongly against the palate. This causes upwards and outwards pressure on the maxilla. The upper dental arch is nudged forwards, to the sides, and upwards by this force.

With an atypical swallow, the face lacks forwards, upwards and outwards pressure. Instead, the maxilla is more likely to narrow and fall down.

By 15 years of age, we have performed a swallow 4 million times. 4 million opportunities to expand the maxilla forwards and laterally, or to offer no expansion at all. Everyone has four million chances, before the sutures of the maxilla and the cheekbones fuse together. Everyone should use those 4 million opportunities to expand the facial bones forwards, outwards and upwards. (See *Figure 40*.)

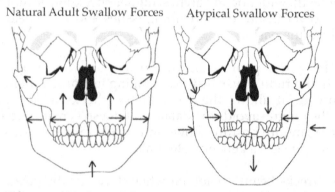

Natural Adult Swallow Forces   Atypical Swallow Forces

Figure 40 – Skull growth directions with natural (left) and unnatural swallowing patterns (right).

There are soft tissue considerations too. Activating cheeks during a swallow makes them fuller. Fuller cheeks eventually sag down your face, as you reach old age, causing jowls. When the whole front of the face is involved with swallowing, the forces are against Nature's expectations.

Swallowing, like breathing and blinking, is something we barely notice. We swallow anywhere between 500 to 900 times per day. How we swallow affects our forward growth, cheeks, and dental arches - and cascades to all other parts of facial beauty.

We have seen the overlap with correct breathing and natural mouth posture. There is also distinct overlap between the development of someone's swallow and *how to eat*.

And now, a warning: This book doesn't concern itself with the ethics of food, nor should it. My interest is in the natural ways our ancestors developed healthily. Ways that have deserted us today. When we think about what is good for facial development, we must consider what people eat and how they eat it. We must also consider the transition from breastfeeding to eating solid foods.

Breastfeeding is discussed and generally encouraged. This is not a political or social statement, merely a developmental one.

Breastfeeding

An infant suckle occurs when a baby breastfeeds. The gums, the tongue, and jaw movement all play their part. In *Figure 41 (overleaf)* you can see the tongue movement - called a *peristaltic wave*. The tongue applies pressure to the nipple from the tip of the tongue (and base of the nipple) to the back of the tongue (and tip of the nipple). Milk is expressed from the nipple by squeezing the nipple against the roof of the baby's mouth using gums and tongue. This wave is the correct way for us all to swallow.

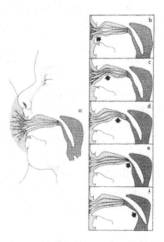

Between each wave, the baby will drop their lower jaw to strengthen the vacuum between the wave movements. Importantly, this movement of the jaw uses the cheek - otherwise called *buccinator* - muscles.

Figure 41 – Peristaltic wave.

The buccinators are active when breastfeeding. Babies don't make side-to-side tongue movements during feeding. These big buccinator muscles keep the tongue centrally aligned when feeding. Adults don't require a vacuum or a nipple to feed and adult tongues move more from side-to-side. The need for big buccinator muscles ends when breastfeeding ends. Hollow cheeks become a sign of a healthy transition from being a baby to being an adult.

Baby cheeks become less "fat" - in reality, less muscular - when the tongue moves side-to-side to break down hard foods, and for advanced speech. It's also an indication of a baby's readiness to wean off breast milk and transition to solid foods. Buccinators naturally lose baby-shape after two years.

Babies throughout history have breastfed for between two and six years. The World Health Organization recommends breastfeeding, *"up to the age of two years or beyond."*[1] Babies should be exclusively breastfed for 6 months, then a child can begin to explore with *solid* foods. The two-year period of babies being exceptionally cute coincides with the length of time that breastfeeding is necessary. The benefits of breastfeeding are:

- Immune support that reflects the environment through mother's milk

- Proper swallow needed to get milk
- Increased bonding between mother and baby
- Natural development of baby
- More likely to adopt proper mouth posture and breathing as a baby
- Retaining full beauty & health potentials

Breastfeeding provides immune system support for babies. A mother passes on antibodies to her baby through breast milk. The milk is tailored to the environment that the baby is born into. Babies who receive this immune support are more likely to have strong immune systems. Babies with strong immune systems are less likely to have autoimmune issues and allergies. In turn, this means they are less likely to mouth breathe. Formula and pureed food do not provide immune support, and encourage a weak, atypical swallow...

Now, for the opposing view. Some babies have intolerances to foods that their mother consumes. This is usually seen on the skin – as rashes or eczema - or by a blocked nose. In those cases, if you want to fully breastfeed, the mother should do an elimination diet to discover which foods are triggering the baby's immune system. Combination feeding breastmilk and formula may also lessen the inflammation, when exclusive breastfeeding proves difficult. Eczema is the first domino to fall in the atopic triad of chronic inflammation. The next is food allergies. Then asthma and hay fever. Stopping this cascade in a baby is vital. If you don't, and they develop allergies, asthma and hayfever, they will likely become a chronic mouth-breather.

Modern Feeding

Bottle feeding, like sucking through a straw, just needs suction. It doesn't require the very specific peristaltic wave and jaw movement. That peristaltic wave is like a dress rehearsal for an adult swallow. The p-wave swallow habit is corrupted when children use a bottle. Bottle feeding isn't the only corruptor of swallowing though. Another culprit is liquified food. I was frequently given pureed baby food from little tins. I remember them well. They were sweet and delicious.

When you break down the fibrous parts of a fruit to make it liquid, sugar hits your body faster. Children and babies love sugar. They demand these pre-packaged products. Parents frequently relent as it keeps their baby happy. Often, because of this, an adult swallow never develops. All our ancestors were able to survive on this earth long enough to reproduce, and all of them, except the last few generations, survived without food processors.

The greatest food processor on earth is your mouth.
The correct way to swallow is to press the tongue against the palate and begin a peristaltic wave. However, babies are typically spoon fed. A spoonful of puree is pushed into their mouths. Parents often try to empty the contents of the spoon in the baby's mouth. Babies instinctively begin the swallow with the spoon *still there*. When a spoon is in the mouth, the swallow is corrupted.

The baby learns not to press against the spoon. Instead, they begin to swallow by sucking the food back. This sucking-swallow, learned from unnatural feeding practices, detracts from the baby's long-term beauty potential. The tongue is underutilized and doesn't swallow in a correct p-wave.

Typically, babies who are spoon-fed dislike feeding. It can be stressful for the parent, who just wants their child to be fed. It's also stressful for the baby, who is given spoonful after spoonful without any choice. It leads to babies learning to activate unnatural tactics to get the food down.

Baby Led Weaning

Children are anatomically ready to eat solid food when their first molars erupt. These are the teeth that crush and liquify food. They erupt between 13-19 months. We tend to ignore this milestone and instead shovel purees into babies' mouths. Predictably, this makes babies difficult to manage and feeding-time highly stressful. Even babies dislike losing their agency.

The shift from a mother's milk to solid food is a shift from an infant swallow to an adult swallow. Yet, the transition to solid food doesn't begin when breastfeeding ends. There should be an overlap. This overlap means that the baby, who continues to use the peristaltic wave when breastfeeding, will also apply it to broken down solid foods. Without that natural overlap, a child is far more likely to fall into bad swallowing habits.

When a baby is about 6 months old, solid foods capture their interest. They want to try what their parents are eating. We have evolved to eat solid foods. I have watched my nephew - aged 8 months - with a carrot stick. He treated it like a dog treats a bone, chewing on it with his gums.

He learned how to pick up the carrot, how to put it in his mouth, the beginnings of how to chew, and how it tasted.

When you put solid foods in front of a baby, they experiment, chew, taste and learn the difference between liquids and solids. Solid food should be served as it is. Blurring the lines between solid food and puree can lead to atypical swallowing.

Puree is not naturally occurring. Water, milk, honey and blood are four naturally occurring liquids that tribes throughout history have consumed. Other forms of sustenance are almost always solid. A baby can figure out how to pick up a small piece of food in front of them and eat it. Babies should discover chewing, taste, look, feel, and hand-to-eye coordination with foods. They should freely choose what to pick up and the senses that it leads to.

Spoon feeding babies puree takes away their curiosity with, and enjoyment of, food. Forcing puree into their mouths leaves an unhappy baby who develops atypical swallowing and chewing habits. Feeding might be less messy with spoons and purees, but that is the only benefit. Easier clean-ups don't benefit your baby at all.

If a child is not ready to eat solid foods, she isn't ready to be weaned off breast milk.

Hollow Cheeks

Hollow cheeks are the result of three things. First, low body-fat. Second, well-defined cheekbones - caused by forward growth. Third, swallowing without using the cheek muscles (buccinators). When someone swallows and the cheeks are very active, the muscles in the cheek grow. Adult swallowing is defined by producing suction with just your tongue. When you don't use your cheeks, the cheek muscles become smaller and hollow cheeks emerge.

Swallowing & Me

I was lying in a dentist's chair when the surgeon asked that I swallow. I did. He nodded; his suspicions confirmed. My swallow used cheeks to channel the saliva. He told me that this is a middle ground between an infant suckle and an adult swallow. An adult swallow only requires movement from the tongue creating firm suction against the roof of the mouth.

And then I remembered, being younger and gulping down a drink at breakfast. My cheeks ballooned with each mouthful, like a hamster hoarding food. The liquid filled my mouth, including between my cheeks and my teeth. My father said, "That's not how you're supposed to drink. Your cheeks shouldn't move." Yet, I believed you are the way you are, and the wind or how you swallow weren't going to change that, thank you very much, Dad.

Yet, how did I develop an atypical swallow? I was fed pureed food when I was young. Pureed apple and banana. Pureed peach and orange. My mealtimes were often made up of very liquid foods, even as I grew older. A soup or a vegetable stew. My swallow never fully transitioned to a strong, powerful adult swallow.

Beauty Quadrant IV: Body Posture (Further Reading)

How Body Posture Affects Facial Development

Unnatural body posture and unnatural mouth posture often occur together. It's no coincidence that those with natural body and mouth posture retain their beauty potential, and those with unnatural body and mouth posture lose it. When your mouth is open, and your tongue is at rest away from your palate the lower jaw falls down and backwards. The back of the tongue retreats slightly into the airway, when natural mouth posture is lost, because even though the jaws are shorter, the tongue isn't smaller. A retreating tongue causes the airway to narrow. (See *Figure 42.*)

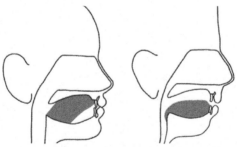

Figure 42 – The tongue doesn't fall into the airway when jaws grow forwards (left), but it does when they are recessed (left). Tongues don't become shorter when jaws are recessed. Instead, they cause the airway to narrow.

The body takes compensatory action when the airway narrows. We thrust the head forwards, causing a curve in the top vertebras of the spine. This makes the airway bigger, to the deficit of natural mouth and body posture. Beauty potential is lost.

A forward head thrust - the face protruding from the spine - doesn't exist in balance. The internal forces which hold up a face with excellent mouth and body posture are compromised when the head projects forwards. When the top few vertebrae of the spine are curved, the weight of the head is amplified. The head goes from about 5.5kg (12 lbs) when properly aligned, to 19 kg (42 lbs) when it protrudes forwards. The strain that this puts on the upper back causes hunchbacks to form. In the face, it causes the maxilla and the lower jaw to fall down and backwards.

When the body is posturally aligned, there is no need for the body to compensate and it's impossible for a hunchback to form. The mouth is closed, the airway is naturally large, the lower jaw and tongue support the natural upwards and outwards growth of the maxilla. The lower jaw follows by growing forwards and out to the sides, rather than sagging downwards. The firm base of strong body posture allows for a firm base of strong mouth posture, so that beauty potential is retained.

Forwards head thrusts that start very young cause huge and obvious facial changes. Where people always point their heads high, the forehead becomes sloped, and the whole face to falls downwards. The neck is curved, the nose appears to be large, and the maxilla and mandible fall way back. When people have weak jaw musculature and unnatural mouth posture, the face grows very long. People who develop a sloped forehead don't have them as babies or very young children. It develops due to unnatural body posture. (See *Figure 43*.)

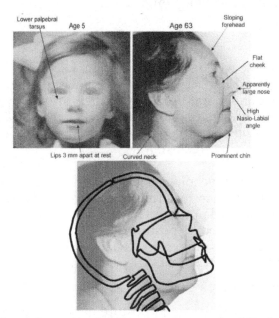

Figure 43 – A 5-year old girl with poor mouth posture (top left) who adopts poor body posture and suffers, at 63 years old, from a sloping forehead, flat cheeks, a large nose, and a curved neck (top right). Overlay of a well-developed skull and spine on her face (below). (Images courtesy of John Mew.)

Other Effects of Body Posture

Poor alignment causes problems in our muscles, our spines and our organs. Improper body posture puts negative pressure on everything, from organs to ligaments, from tendons to joints. Even tension headaches are caused by this imbalance. The whole body is affected.

However, sit and stand as nature intends and your stomach has space to digest properly. Your lungs have space to fully expand. The body is more relaxed and calmer. This leads to some extraordinary benefits. Learning and memory are improved by good posture. Efficiencies compound to cause significant natural benefits. Inefficiencies compound to cause lost potentials.

And what of physicality? Standing tall and having head, shoulders, spine and hips in alignment looks more attractive. Good posture makes people perceive you as more confident, competent and strong. High-status individuals project their high status through body language and body posture. Physiology and psychology influence each other in a virtuous circle. If you think powerfully, physiology improves. If you stand powerfully, psychology improves.

Physiology <-> Psychology

Soldiers around the world stand upright and tall. There is good reason for this. Physiology impacts psychology and standing tall improves decision-making and morale. Slouchy soldiers are sloppy soldiers. This has been innately understood for thousands of years. Standing tall has always been instilled in successful armies. Modern science is finally beginning to show why: Testosterone.

Amy Cuddy, social psychologist and author of *Presence*, writes that "power" poses increase testosterone and decrease cortisol in the body. Power poses are tall and upright. They project confidence. It only takes minutes of improved body posture to reduce cortisol and increase testosterone. The effects of increased testosterone and reduced cortisol include being more ready to take risks, being more proactive and being more assertive.

It's key with body language and posture to be comfortable taking up space. Trying to slouch yourself into non-existence negatively affects how people perceive you, the chemicals in your body, your mood, your confidence, energy levels, even the chance of a soldier's survival.

Breathing & Body Posture

Scientists have been able to measure the effect of different postures on breathing. When seated, the very worst posture for efficient breathing is slouching. Next is sitting with a straight back. Better still is sitting with lumbar support. Standing straight beats all the above. The best posture for efficient breathing is the posture that projects most trust in others. Standing tall is better than being hunched.

This all fits with the *Theory of Propinquity* which is not only based on facial structure and facial posture, but also on body posture. It comes as little surprise that those with the best posture tend to be those who are the most facially attractive. This is for a few significant reasons. The head is always in proper alignment with the body. Sex hormones are released to their maximum potential during puberty, making men look more masculine and women more feminine. Muscles stay balanced, from the face and neck muscles, down to your feet. Natural body posture also makes maintaining natural mouth posture easier.

Body Posture & Me

When I was at school, a physical education teacher who I had a good relationship with told me as we walked to the cafeteria that my shoulders were slumped over, "Stand up tall!" From that day forth, I did. However, I still slouched in chairs.

Since smartphones became ubiquitous, we slump over our screens. Even as we walk, we bend our necks to read our phones. Daily posture has declined in ways that nature didn't expect. Stone Age man would walk for miles. Head, shoulders, spine and hips in alignment. They'd look directly forwards, scanning the landscape. This is what nature intends and expects. Deviation away from this causes the face to develop wrongly.

How the Face Grows

The face is the most changeable part of the human body, and the part of the head that grows the most outside the womb. This growth occurs as we interact with the environment in complex ways. It is shaped by resting mouth posture, how we consume food and drink, swallowing, body posture (Beauty Quadrant) and our levels of inflammation (Health Quadrant.) This complexity can cause lots of deviation from ideal growth.

Faces can become many different shapes and proportions. These changes occur incrementally and become more obvious as we reach adulthood.

Why Do All Babies Have The Same Facial Proportions?

All babies have very similar, ideal facial proportions in their first 6 months of life. They all have flat faces, big eyes, flat and short eyebrows, chubby cheeks, slightly retruded lower jaws, small and upturned noses, and small faces in proportion to their heads. The babies who become beautiful adults are proportionally very similar in early life to the babies who become less attractive adults. All babies are similarly cute. Their features - such as skin, hair and eye colour - differ greatly but their proportions do not.

Before complex environmental forces can change how the face develops, our proportions are predictable. I challenge anyone to find a healthy baby with a long, thin face. Or with a downturned nose with a dorsal hump in the middle. Or a protruding lower jaw. Good luck - they don't exist!

Babies haven't had a chance to lose their beauty potential, because environments haven't had a chance to change their facial structure yet. Some faces - beautiful ones - retain "cute" proportions through to adulthood. Most faces don't.

Remember: Faces lose ideal proportions through the *degree* and *duration* of unnatural pressure. The physical environment in the womb is virtually identical for all babies, which is why they all emerge with almost identical facial proportions. Their beauty potential - their potential to retain ideal proportions - is fully intact at birth.

A baby's face will lose ideal proportions only when they;

1, Leave the womb.

2, Stray from the expected, natural environmental forces of the *Beauty Quadrant* that shape the face.

Post-birth environmental pressures have exponentially more variety than a womb's environment. This is why adult facial proportions are so much more variable than baby facial proportions. While all babies share the same proportions, by adulthood proportions can vary wildly as facial forces take hold.

All healthy babies are born with the potential to retain their cuteness, straying from the *Beauty & Health Quadrants* snatches away those potentials, replacing them with vulnerabilities.

Vulnerabilities are worrying for both beauty and long-term health. Yet, these facts offer a slice of hope for humanity. Realising our beauty and health potentials is our birth right.

Facial Growth From Birth To Adulthood

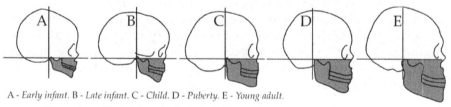

A - *Early infant*. B - *Late infant*. C - *Child*. D - *Puberty*. E - *Young adult*.

Figure 44 – Facial growth through childhood. Note how much the face grows compared to the rest of the head.

From under the eye, out to the cheekbones, down to the lower jaw, the facial bones exist. The relative growth of these bones compared with the rest of the skull, between birth and adulthood, is astonishing.

A baby's face endures incredible growth into adulthood. It's the part of the skull which does the most growing post-birth. (See *Figure 44*.) In early infancy, the face makes up about 13% of a head in profile. By early adulthood, it's more than doubled to 30%. If anywhere on the body is likely to be shaped by environments, it's here. And we don't have to go through skull records for all the clues that environmental forces shape the face.

Asymmetry Shows That Facial Forces Matter

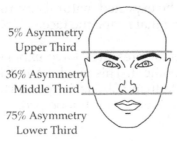

5% Asymmetry
Upper Third

36% Asymmetry
Middle Third

75% Asymmetry
Lower Third

Figure 45 – Where asymmetry occurs on the face.

If we claimed that facial proportions were genetically predetermined, and not shaped by environments, asymmetry would be evenly distributed across the face. If it's shaped by environments, asymmetry would appear at the complex moving parts; more around the mouth - which deals with breathing, eating, drinking and talking forces - than, say, around the eyebrows - which deal with far fewer forces.

The data[1] shows the impact of facial forces on asymmetry. (See *Figure 45*.) There is least asymmetry in the top third of the face (5%) where there are few complex movements, more in the middle third (36%) which requires mouth posture to grow proportionally, and the most in the lower third (75%) with its vast complexity of eating, swallowing, talking and mouth posture differences. The parts of the face that are more active - that can be held and moved in complex ways - are asymmetry hotspots.

Direct Facial Forces Impact Facial Development

As a baby's face grows, direct forces shape it. Babies have soft bones at birth. As we age, they become more difficult to shape. When we are very old, they become brittle.

The cranial sutures in the skull define our proportions and must be nudged and gently pried apart by natural, expected forces. These are the points where the different bones meet. When these bones are slowly pulled apart by a growing head and natural mouth posture, swallowing and chewing, new bone grows along the suture lines.

These natural environmental forces on the face lead to the forwards and lateral facial growth that makes us healthier and more beautiful. Faces can only retain their proportions when these natural forces cause facial bones to be gently pulled apart each day by the Beauty Quadrant tenets. The shapes of facial bones change based on these pressures.

Let's take an obvious example. Long-term pacifier use or thumb-sucking changes the shape of a young person's jaws. 71% of children who suck their thumb past the age of 4 have malocclusion, compared to 14% who stop the habit at 24 months.[2] Faces continue to grow and to be shaped until the cranial sutures fuse at about 15 years old.

This research highlights two key points, however: First, the younger we are, the more we can be shaped. If a 25-year-old started sucking their thumb, we wouldn't worry about changes to their jaws. Second, failure to maintain correct mouth posture is shown to cause malocclusion and unnatural facial growth.

Hierarchy of Survival - What We Need to Consume

Our environments - that we're so expert at changing - also change us. Shifts from hunting to farming, then from farms to factories, saw the biggest changes in facial form, for three reasons: 1, we consumed things differently, and we consumed different things, 2, we became more chronically inflamed by our new environments and consumption habits, 3, we formed new, negative habits – like mouth breathing.

Generally speaking, the more we change our environments, the more we are changed by them. Consumption is tremendously important for direct Beauty Quadrant forces on the face and for indirect Health Quadrant forces that affect levels of chronic inflammation.

In 1943 American psychologist Abraham Maslow published a paper called *A Theory of Human Motivation*. His paper included a pyramid of what motivates people's decisions, called Maslow's *Hierarchy of Needs*. I'd like to propose a new hierarchy for beauty and health; the *Hierarchy of Survival*. It's the story of consumption.

We need to *consume* things to survive another minute, day, week or month. How we consume each profoundly affects facial development. Consumption is where our environment interacts with, shapes, and becomes part of us. It's where Nature's environmental expectations are fulfilled or unmet. Consume the wrong thing, or the right thing in the wrong way, and beauty potential is lost.

Let's start with the most immediately important consumable…

Air

Breathing is the most important act of consumption we take every single day. We can survive just minutes without air. How we breathe and the amount we breathe can dramatically affect inflammation and facial development. Breathing is mostly unconscious. We therefore assume that we breathe the right amount, in the right way, instinctively. This is false.

Breathing efficiency is vital to retaining beauty and health potentials. If you mouth-breathe, your potentials always slip away. If you nose breathe exclusively, they can be retained.

Air forms the base of our *Hierarchy of Survival:*

Water

Water is the second most important consumable after air. Have too little or too much water and you will die. People can survive without water for between 2 days to a week, depending on factors including the ambient temperature and exposure to direct sunlight.

Drinking is active. The main action required to drink, swallowing, occurs hundreds of times per day, even when we aren't drinking. Here is our pyramid so far:

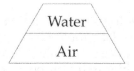

Food

We must consume, and love consuming, food to survive. How much and the types of food we eat shape our health and longevity. How we eat – how hard the food is, how much we chew it and break it down – shapes the face. If we are prone to inflammation, what we eat and when we eat can lose both beauty and health potentials.

Food, therefore, belongs on our *Hierarchy of Survival:*

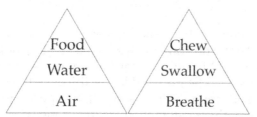

Figure 46 – The Hierarchy of Survival (left) and the forces for each level (right)

The Hierarchy Reflects Acts Of Consumption

The physiological forces of how you breathe, swallow, eat and drink define your beauty. When these processes occur as nature intended, we retain our potentials. Any deviation away from this causes facial disproportion. The *Hierarchy of Survival* highlights where beauty and health are retained or lost.

Every facial force shapes a child's face by tiny amounts, which compounds positively or negatively to retain or lose facial proportion and symmetry.

Where Beauty Exists

It's interesting to see an overlay of where the things we consume physically interact with the face. The first contact of the elements in the *Hierarchy of Survival* occurs from the top of the nose to the chin.

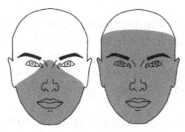

Figure 47 – Hierarchy of Survival area for breathing, eating and drinking (left). Where beauty occurs (right).

The key zone for facial beauty runs from our hair down to our chin. The width and length of our faces, and all the features within that area define our beauty.

Facial beauty occurs in the exact places where consumption begins. (See *Figure* 47.) That's no coincidence. To steal a technology phrase; it's a feature, not a bug. Living in accordance with Nature's expectations leads to facial beauty. The mid and lower thirds of the face are the most changeable parts of the face, the parts that require most growth from birth to adulthood, the most likely to grow wrong when environmental expectations are unmet, and the most important for how beautiful and healthy you are. Beauty occurs in this area of just a handful of bones.

The Beauty Bones

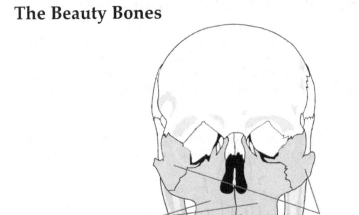

Figure 48 – The bones that define facial beauty.

The bones that define beauty are the gateways to consumption. (See *Figure 48.*) The **maxilla**, in the middle of the face, is the dominant facial bone. The **mandible**; the lower jawbone. The **zygomatic** bones - the cheekbones - which are propped up by the maxilla and connected to the mandible by the largest chewing muscles, the masseters.

Let's look at each set of bones from top to bottom of the face.

The Zygomatics

The cheekbones (zygomatic bones) support half of the under-eye area, define the width of the midface, and are a vital component of facial beauty.

The cheekbones sit on the maxilla. When the maxilla grows more forwards, the cheekbones project forwards and higher. When the maxilla grows wider, the cheekbones are pushed further apart. High, wide set cheekbones are considered highly attractive. They give more space behind them for your nasal cavity - crucial for breathing health.

The Maxilla

The maxilla is the dominant facial bone. It's far and away the most important bone for beauty. It sits in the middle of the face, and it dictates how the mandible and cheekbones grow around it. Where the maxilla leads, those other bones follow.

The maxilla grows forwards and laterally when passive and active forces are applied; natural mouth posture, a fully developed adult swallow, and lots of tearing, biting, and chewing tough food. These pressures expand the maxilla at its sutures. Forwards growth gives more space for your teeth, the nasal cavity, your maxillary sinuses, and your upper airway.

The maxilla guides lower jaw growth - provided you apply natural mouth posture at rest. When the mouth is open, the lower jaw isn't guided by the upper jaw.

The cheekbones grow high and wide when the maxilla grows forwards and laterally. Or narrow set, flat and downwards when the maxilla isn't supported by natural mouth posture and strong chewing muscles.

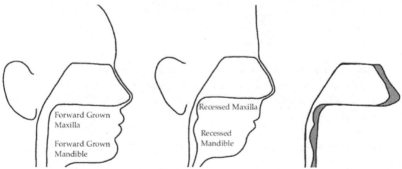

Figure 49 – A well-developed face maintains a large nasal cavity and upper airway (left). Recessed jaws lead to a smaller nasal cavity and bottlenecks in the upper airway (center). An overlay of a large upper airway versus a small one (right) – shaded grey area is the extra space for a well-developed face.

Sharp-eyed readers will have noticed that the maxilla is two bones connected in the centre of the face by a vertical cranial suture. It, therefore, grows wider under the right pressures. It also contains its own cranial sutures in the palate (the roof of the mouth.)

The nose, the beginning of the airway, and the upper part of the mouth are housed in the maxilla. The maxilla is central to all the levels on the *Hierarchy of Survival*; it's involved in eating, drinking and breathing. Most importantly, the airway takes up a vast, central clump of the human head. From under the eyes to the roof of the mouth, the nose, nasal cavity and maxillary sinuses exist. They are shaped by maxilla development, and the cheekbones around it.

The nasal cavity and maxillary sinuses should be as horizontally deep and wide as possible. This requires lots of forwards and lateral growth of the maxilla. More space is always better for nasal passages, so that they can filter, warm and humidity air efficiently.

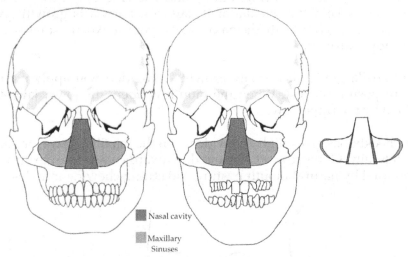

Figure 50 - Comparison of well-proportioned face (left) and poorly proportioned face (center). An overlay of nasal cavity and sinus size between well-developed and poorly-developed face (right) — shaded grey area is the extra space for a well-developed face.

The upper jaw's arch depth and width forms the base of the nasal cavity.

Maximum nasal cavity volume isn't just defined by the upper dental arch. Moving up the mid-third of the face, the cheekbones should be high, forward projected and wide set so the nasal cavity and the maxillary sinuses reach optimal volume. A face with wide, forward grown nasal passages is more beautiful and healthier, and the maxilla should grow forwards and wide.

An unsupported maxilla grows downwards, backwards and more narrow.

The Mandible

The mandible (lower jaw) follows the maxilla consistently when natural mouth posture is maintained, but very inconsistently when mouth posture isn't maintained. For this reason, mouth breathers often lose far more beauty potential than nose breathers, through a recessed or protruding lower jaw.

The lower jaw offers support for the upper jaw so that the maxilla can grow forwards and laterally, rather than sagging down. When the upper jaw is recessed, the lower jaw is often recessed too. The mandible is connected to the zygomatic bones through the masseter muscles. These are the main muscles used to bite and chew food. Stronger bite force is associated with shorter, wider faces.

The upper and lower jaws are guided into position passively by natural mouth posture, by actively by biting, tearing and chewing tough foods, and by swallowing. The chewing muscles add to the support of the upper jaw by being strong and well-developed. A strong jaw develops when it is well used.

Faces Can Grow in Many Different Ways – Only One of Them Is Optimal

The face can lose proportion in many ways.

Long Face Syndrome: Faces that don't adhere to the Beauty Quadrant get longer. At the extreme, this becomes long face syndrome. However, there are degrees of face lengthening. This lengthening doesn't occur equally in each third. Typically, the lower third is most affected, the mid third can be affected too. The upper third can be slightly affected, when sloping foreheads develop, for example.

All faces should grow forwards and laterally, as touching upper and lower teeth, strong masseter muscles, and a strong tongue in the palate halt downwards growth. When faces don't grow forwards and laterally, the only way to grow is down. This always causes disproportion. Faces that grow down become narrower as well as longer. This narrowing can occur at the cheekbones, the maxilla and the mandible.

The maxilla, which houses the upper teeth, drops and falls backwards. This risks excessive tooth display and gummy smiles. The front upper and lower teeth can form an open bite, where they don't touch when the back teeth are touching. The mandibular plane, as we've already seen, becomes steeper.

An Undeveloped Maxilla: The midface becomes deficient when the maxilla is underdeveloped – lacking forwards and lateral growth. This gives a flat midface profile. (See *Figure 51.*)

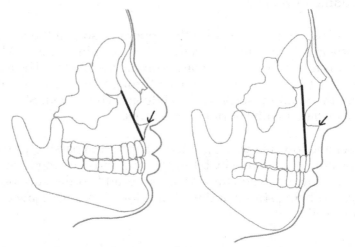

Figure 51 - Black line shows a more forwards grown, shorter midface (left) and a flatter, longer midface (left). Arrow shows anterior nasal spine.

Undereye support is lost from the maxilla and the cheekbones. The cheekbones become narrower and downward grown. This changes the canthal tilt of the eyes (See *Figure 52.*) and can result in scleral show. It also makes the nose look bigger. Most people who believe they have big noses actually don't. They have a recessed maxilla. The nose looks bigger because the maxilla sinks back. It's like measuring the height of a tree after removing a foot of soil from its base.

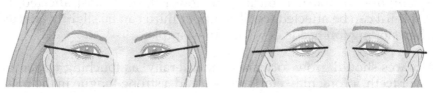

Figure 52 - Positive canthal tilt, where the outer corner of the eye is higher than the inner corner (left). Negative canthal tilt, where the reverse is true (right).

When the maxilla rotates clockwise, the anterior nasal spine, which offers support for the nose, is set back. (See arrows in *Figure 51.*) This can cause a hump in the nose as there is less support for the bottom half of it. Narrow cheekbones and maxillae cause a narrower upper airway and nasal cavity, which makes breathing less efficient.

A narrow maxilla, as discussed previously, leaves far less room for teeth. They emerge crowded, crooked, and potentially impacted. People need wisdom tooth extractions because their maxilla doesn't develop fully.

Other potential issues with an underdeveloped maxilla are crossbites (where the lower teeth emerge outside the upper teeth) or an underbite, where the front lower teeth are further forward than front upper teeth. Underbites occur when the tongue rests between the lower teeth, guiding lower jaw growth in place of the maxilla.

A Recessed Lower Jaw: The lower jaw (the mandible) can grow in a few ways. In disproportional faces, it's either recessed or it protrudes too much. An underdeveloped jaw causes a receding chin, a convex facial profile, and a short lower third of the face. For lower teeth, expect an overbite – where the front teeth are too far in front of the lower teeth - or an overjet - where there is horizontal distance between the lower front teeth and the upper front teeth. And you get crookedness, crowding and impacted teeth.

An Overdeveloped Lower Jaw: When the lower jaw is overdeveloped – because the tongue habitually rests between the lower teeth - a concave facial profile forms. The lower third of the face is typically far more vertically grown. The teeth can form an underbite and a crossbite.

Asymmetry: The jaws growing unevenly is one form of asymmetry caused by uneven mouth posture, uneven swallowing, chewing on one dominant side, tilting the head to one side, on sleeping on one side of the face.

Facial asymmetry is caused by the same issues, which can cause one or more of the facial bones to be affected. This can also lead to a deviated septum, when the maxilla is recessed. The maxilla is two bones attached in the centre by a vertical maxillary suture, and each side can grow in different ways, when each side receives different environmental pressures.

Crossbites – where the upper teeth occlude outside their corresponding lower teeth – are common for asymmetry. Sometimes you also get a tilted occlusal plane. This occurs when you hold a pencil between your jaws, and it is not horizontal when your head is perfectly upright.

Oral Facial Deficiencies: When the maxilla drops and the intermolar width is small, you get a narrow upper dental arch and, often, a high palatal vault. You also get a crossbite at the back of the teeth. Teeth also become crowded and impacted.

All these issues can be avoided when young people adopt the Beauty Quadrant and ensure that their Health Quadrant supports it.

Part II: The Health Quadrant: Chronic Inflammation

Part I of this book focuses on the direct physical forces of the Beauty Quadrant that shape facial development. We have agency over how we hold our faces and bodies, how we eat, and how we swallow. While unnatural habits form, we can train ourselves out of them, just as we may have unwittingly trained ourselves into them. Those physical forces act *directly* to retain or lose out beauty potential. Once we understand what these forces are, it is obvious when they occur wrongly.

Part II of this book focuses on forces that work indirectly and either support or undermine the Beauty Quadrant. They are more stealthy and less obvious, in part because they act indirectly. We should optimise our Health Quadrant so that it naturally supports the Beauty Quadrant, and for long-term health. Unfortunately, for many of us, a weak Health Quadrant undermines our ability to consistently apply the four pillars of the Beauty Quadrant, and we therefore lose both our beauty and health potentials.

Whereas Part I affects everyone, Part II only affects those prone to inflammation. This means for a few readers, Part II is not a concern. For many, it is. The only way to be sure is to take an inflammation test. I recommend some accurate tests on my website.

John Mew's Children Experiments

John Mew is the father of Orthotropics, which focuses on growing forward, wide jaws and beautiful, harmonious faces. *The New York Times Magazine* ran a piece about Mew. It details the experiments he conducted on his own children when testing his Orthotropic premise. Orthotropics failed for Bill, Mew's first child, because Bill suffered from severe allergies and couldn't keep his mouth shut. Mew even resorted to hypnosis to try to fix this. It failed.

Mew's third child, Rosie, was given a fully liquid diet for the first 4 years of her life as an opposite experiment: What would happen if you did the reverse of the Orthotropic method, which promotes chewing tough food? The results were awful. Rosie said, in her own words: *"I had teeth growing one in front of the other... I was a really, really ugly little kid."*[1] A liquid-only diet and unnatural mouth posture meant that her teeth and facial development were a mess as early as age 4.

Mew's second child, Mike, achieved his Orthotropic ambitions. The article described the difference between John's face and Mike's: *"Where John's face is thin and oblong, Mike's is wide and short, his chewing muscles so large that you can see them flex."*[2] Mike Mew has a strong jawline because he had good mouth posture; chewed tough food growing up and developed an adult swallow; *and* had low enough levels of inflammation to maintain natural mouth posture.

Mike's facial development is optimal because his Beauty Quadrant was optimal, and his Health Quadrant didn't interfere with it. Rosie's Beauty Quadrant was deliberately sabotaged. Bill's Beauty Quadrant was unwittingly sabotaged by his weak Health Quadrant. Orthotropics doesn't acknowledge the *chronic inflammation problem*. Mew's success rate was only 50% with his own sons. His experiments on his children reveal that reducing chronic inflammation is key for consistent results.

John Mew doesn't include biting and tearing in his tropic premise. I believe that biting and tearing food is a key component for maximising forwards facial growth.

The inconsistent results of Orthotropics can be corrected in the Health Quadrant chapters of this book. For children who already mouth-breathe, stamping out the inflammation and the habit are necessary.

The Potentials Killer

Chronic inflammation corrupts beauty and health potentials. This corruption comes from consumables - food and air. Most chronic inflammation is caused by inflammatory foods and overbreathing, which often occur together. When natural mouth posture is replaced by mouth breathing, the face deviates from optimal proportions, symmetry and sexual dimorphism.

Four Immune Systems in The Body

The body contains a collective of four immune systems. The biggest is your gut, which accounts for approximately 70-85% of your total immunity. The liver contains Kupffer cells, which account for some more. White blood cells in the blood are another. And the brain contains the rest, in its glial cells. These act as one team, not individual entities. When there is an insult to one part of the immune system, the immune system as a whole is ready to fight.

The only tools in your immune system's arsenal are cytokines and antibodies. Cytokines are the first line of defence. When they fail, antibodies are called upon. We have the same immune system as our ancient ancestors, yet we are faced with far more insults: pollution, toxic chemicals, heavy metals, modern grains, sugars, and (for many) dairy.

When cytokines have inflamed an area, but their attack fails, antibodies are released. Antibodies are a more potent attack. Antibodies, in turn, release an abundance of histamines. Histamines are a sign of allergy and can be deadly for some.

The immune system remembers threats, but the memory can fade (which is why we have booster shots for certain vaccinations.) This memory serves us well with diseases. The body can swiftly identify and target a virus that we've had before. The downside is that when we have repeated exposure to something like gluten or pollen, our immune system remembers. As it tries to kill the threat, real damage to healthy tissues can continuously occur, as antibodies go on seek and destroy missions throughout the body and cause collateral damage to nearby healthy cells. This accrued damage to healthy cells leads to more obvious and more severe issues over time.

Take gluten - a well-known insult. The implications of repeated exposure were revealed in *The Lancet* for people who suffer with Celiac disease: *"Non-adherence to the GFD [Gluten Free Diet], defined as eating gluten once per month, increased the relative risk of death sixfold."*[3] For people whose immune system goes into hyperdrive when gluten is present, just one slice of bread a month can increase mortality by an incredible amount. This is due to the damage that antibodies wreak on healthy cells throughout the body. The accrued damage destroys health and longevity.

Celiac disease is at the very far end of the autoimmune spectrum. Yet, everyone who ignores an intolerance is threatening their health. Continued elevation of seek-and-destroy antibodies leads to inflammation and tissue damage. Antibodies are less sniper rifle, more shotgun. They don't just take out the "bad guy," they cause lots of collateral damage too. When you are constantly fighting triggers in the body, you begin an autoimmune cascade, where the immune system is perpetually fighting and doing damage to healthy cells throughout the body. This is autoimmunity; the body attacking itself.

Three Pillars of Most Chronic Diseases

In his book, *The Autoimmune Fix*, Tom O'Bryan proposes that three prongs are required to get onto the autoimmune spectrum:

1. Vulnerability (the genetic, or epigenetic component)

2. Trigger (the insult: what the immune system attacks your body)

3. Intestinal Permeability (the straw that breaks the camel's back)

These three prongs, occurring in unison, lead to a gradual accumulation of damage that leads to chronic or deadly disease. For facial development, you don't need to reach the far end of the spectrum to create an environment where beauty potential can be lost. A blocked nose which causes the mouth to drop open can cause the habit of mouth breathing can stick, causing the face to grow downwards instead of forwards.

But remember, you don't need to be on the autoimmune spectrum to mouth breathe. However, being on the autoimmune spectrum increases the probability of mouth breathing significantly.

The inflammatory cascade starts without obvious symptoms. This stage is called benign autoimmunity. Damage begins to accumulate slightly further up the spectrum at the stage called pathogenic autoimmunity. Damage builds consistently when you don't stamp insults out. At the most dangerous end of the scale, you see disease or clinical illness. Anyone genetically susceptible to autoimmune issues, who is exposed to the trigger, and has intestinal permeability, will have heightened antibodies in their blood. These antibodies damage healthy cells throughout your body.

Different people on the autoimmune spectrum have their own different point - or points - of weakness. Imagine all the systems in your body as links on a chain. When you pull the chain of your body, the weak link(s) will break. That weakest link is where you will first feel inflammation. For some, this will be hay fever, for others it may be lupus. A whole myriad of health issues, which can't yet be diagnosed as a disease by doctors, are clues to take evasive measures before inflammation turns to chronic disease. Many chronic diseases occur because of repeated autoimmune damage triggered by inflammatory foods and overbreathing.

Symptoms of autoimmune problems can include things that appear to be unrelated: Bloating, fatigue, headaches, memory lapses, rashes, haemorrhoids, ganglions or joint pain can point to an underlying autoimmune issue. These problems surface when you reach the *final* straw in the three pillars of most chronic diseases, not before! I repeat, these problems occur only when you are far along the path to chronic disease! From this point forward, unless you act, damage will accumulate until you're diagnosed with a disease.

For some there is one weak link - where an illness seemingly appears out of nowhere. For others there are many weak links - where illnesses stack on top of one another and someone is perpetually, chronically ill. Brushing these problems off, or taking mild painkillers to disguise the problems, only leads to more damage.

If autoimmunity develops after a child has reached the age of 15 years or so, then their beauty potential is less likely to be compromised. Yet the slow march of health declines - often wrongly put down to ageing - will continue. To stop this decline, remove the insult, breathe efficiently, repair the gut and only eat foods that your body isn't triggered by.

Resetting your air efficiency and your gut microbiome are key to halting the march towards autoimmune crises and chronic diseases. The pathway - from cell damage to tissue damage, to organ inflammation, to organ damage, to physical symptoms, to diagnosed disease - is clear. As with facial development, the sooner you change the environmental factors leading to this decline, and the less severe these factors are, the better off you will be. Your gut, and its permeability, play a huge role in this.

I once met someone who ate a sandwich, then fell into a thorny bush, causing cuts all over their body. After this event, they became gluten intolerant. The immune system linked gluten to the cuts and forever sought to eliminate gluten. Inflammation somewhere can cause an intolerance to something seemingly unrelated. The only defence is eliminating any inflammatory foods and efficient breathing.

British cardiologist Claude Lum says of overbreathing; it *"presents a collection of bizarre and often apparently unrelated symptoms, which may affect any part of the body, and any organ or any system."*[4] These effects of air inefficiency are the same as of food intolerances.

No Cell Is Safe

When the body is inflamed in one place (such as the airway), it is more likely to be inflamed everywhere.

If your kitchen is shaken by an earthquake, your whole house will be too!

When the gut wall is permeable *and* triggers are running rampant in the airway, the gut and the bloodstream, no cell is safe. Gluten *always* causes holes in the gut. Some people remain unaffected, as they are not genetically vulnerable. Their immune systems ignore the insult and have no memory of it causing damage. However, for a vast proportion of the population, the immune system is constantly fighting.

When under-digested, large blocks of food breaks through the gut wall holes, directly into the blood stream, the immune system fights it with antibodies, through white blood cells. When the bloodstream becomes contaminated by immune system triggers, you have a huge problem. Blood goes almost everywhere. Which means collateral damage can occur everywhere. Nowhere is safe from damage.

The mystifying thing about beauty is how every part of exceptionally beautiful people appears to be optimal. The face, skin, hair, scent, even how shiny and bright their eyes are. In inflamed people, everything can become damaged. Now we can see why. Inflamed bodies tend to be inflamed - to greater or lesser extents - in *any* cells. Some areas are a weak link. Other areas are less damaged. But damage accrues all over when we allow inflammation to thrive. Different people have different weak links. However, usually, every cell is affected to a certain extent when a body is inflamed.

Let's zoom in. Imagine you are a tiny part of the body, pushing out a single strand of hair. You sit below the top layer of skin. You are surrounded by blood vessels, nerves, a sebaceous gland, a sweat gland, and the dermal papilla. You keep your strand of hair growing each day. Yet, all the blood that comes to nourish you causes inflammation. The blood carries triggers from a gut barrier breach, and there is a battle in your tiny part of the body. A blood vessel is damaged by an antibody, the sebaceous gland is damaged, the skin that your hair strand sprouts through is damaged. Suddenly, a consistent, smooth strand of hair becomes a damaged, weak strand of hair. Maybe it's too oily, maybe to dry. This tiny part of the body isn't the only area affected. Every strand is subjected to the same risks. Now zoom out. It's not just hair or skin, it's joints, tendons, muscles, and organs, including the brain. It's every part of you. Every cell can become pockmarked with collateral damage. Everything then develops sub optimally.

When there is no inflammation, there is no deviation from our optimal health potential.

Take skin. You could have oily or dry skin which develops into acne, eczema or psoriasis. It could fade and leave no lasting damage. Yet, the longer you have it, and the greater its severity, the more likely you are to suffer from life-long scarring. It can occur as acne scars or thinner skin. In the short term, inflammation can disappear. On a long enough timeline, inflammation causes damage that is irreversible, in any organ at any time, when chronic inflammation is free to reign.

The Atopic Triad – Eczema, Food Allergies, Asthma & Hay Fever

The worst chronic inflammation issue for beauty potential is the atopic triad. It starts as eczema, then food allergies, then hay fever and asthma emerge. This is so disastrous because airway inflammation often causes mouth breathing. These issues can snowball quickly, and the common response means that most people accept it, live with it, and take no dietary interventions to eradicate it. That response? *"It's genetic."*

Genetics is one of three factors that causes autoimmunity to exist. The others – a trigger, and gut permeability – must also be present for the atopic triad to take hold. There are people in the world with the genetic vulnerability, who have never suffered from chronic inflammation because they aren't exposed to a trigger, or they don't have gut permeability, or both of those.

To remove the risk, you must eliminate the trigger(s) and gut permeability.

Testosterone & Estrogen Ranges

Scientists have long known the association between sex hormones and facial attractiveness. However, they tend to imply that sex hormones cause attractiveness. i.e., Beautiful women have more oestrogen, so oestrogen causes beauty in women. This is the cart leading the horse. Epigenetic gene-regulation dictates how much testosterone (for men) or estrogen (for women) is released during puberty. Those who receive the environmental expectations found in the *Beauty & Health Quadrants* get higher levels – within their genetic range – of sex hormones at the onset of puberty and beyond.

Women get more oestrogen and look more feminine, having smaller noses and lower jaws, bigger eyes, fuller lips. Men get a thicker brow, a wider jaw, higher brow ridges, and more prominent cheekbones.

Studies show that high testosterone weakens the immune system.[5] Sex hormones themselves are a liability. Gene regulation selects more sex hormones for the efficient, less-inflamed person, and fewer sex hormones for the less efficient, more-inflamed person. How much depends on how efficient and healthy the person is as puberty commences. The body selects how much sex hormones based on how inflamed we are.

Inflammation Delays Maturity

Asthmatics, and those with inflamed bodies, get levels of sex hormones at the lower end their genetic range. This makes sense.

However, the body doesn't just reduce sex hormones in inflamed people, it *delays* puberty. Puberty for asthmatics is delayed by 1.3 years.[6] This drastic decision underlines how much the body fights to optimise beauty and health potentials. Puberty is put on hold in the hope of resolving inflammation before it locks in how much sex hormone to release. It's a last-ditch roll of the dice.

Non-inflamed bodies not only get more sex hormones, but they also get them sooner. Inflamed bodies are given as much opportunity as possible to resolve inflammation by finding better environments before the onset of puberty.

Modern asthmatics have little chance of dramatically reducing inflammation (unless they become more efficient with air and remove all inflammatory foods.) Typically, after delaying for as long as possible in the hope of reducing inflammation, the body is forced to select sex hormone "dosage" at the lower end of its range. The body, at this stage, won't risk extreme sexual dimorphism; high dose sex hormones. In this way, beauty potential is forever lost at a critical point in facial development.

Non-Facial Potentials

Beautiful hair, or skin, or glimmering eyes occur because of low inflammation. Young children all have beautiful hair. Why do some retain healthy hair as others lose it? Because at the onset of puberty they are virtuously supported by, or viciously undermined by, the amount of sex hormones our bodies produce. Sex hormones are released in low quantities in the inflamed and in high quantities in those without inflammation. If your body is inflamed and hair or skin are weak links, they will accrue visible damage.

Puberty compounds beauty in the less inflamed; and it compounds beauty loss in the more inflamed. In certain ways, such as facial bones, this is locked in forever. In other ways, like skin health or how people smell, it is more changeable. People high in sex hormones smell more attractive. Inflammation inhibits non-facial potentials, such as smell, skin, or hair. Inflamed cells produce less attractive parts of us and a less attractive whole.

Sporting Evidence

A more efficient facial structure leads to better overall efficiency. It also leads to better performance. This is observable by looking at explosive athletes - 100-meter runners or boxers - and seeing how many have jaw recession. In champions, jaw recession is virtually non-existent. An association has been found between facial width-to-height ratio (fWHR) and fighting ability among male mixed martial artists. The hypothesis is that increased testosterone leads to wider faces and greater fWHR, which leads to increased aggression. However, as discussed, I believe that the release of testosterone is *increased* during puberty when function and facial form are optimal. When inflammation is very low and facial form is optimal, breathing is more efficient, and more sex hormone is selected for. More testosterone allows for more muscle mass. When two athletes who train in exactly the same way have different testosterone levels, the higher testosterone male has an advantage. Combine this muscular advantage with a more efficient respiratory system and it's clear why they become champions.

Health Quadrant I: Breathing (Further Reading)

Breathing & The Maxilla

In the *Hierarchy of Survival* pyramid the most significant level is air. Its presence is necessary for each of the half-billion breaths you take in your lifetime.

The nasal passages are designed to filter out all the filth from the air, to warm it, and to humidify it. They also, unlike the mouth, limit breathing volume. When you breathe naturally and efficiently, the lungs receive clean, temperature-controlled, humid air in the right quantity. Naturally prepared air reduces the chance of respiratory inflammation dramatically.

The upper dental arch is the base of the nasal cavity. When the upper dental arch is underdeveloped, the nasal cavity is underdeveloped. When the cheekbones and maxilla don't project upwards and outwards, and instead sink down and fall into the face, the whole nasal cavity and maxillary sinuses are squeezed and have less volume to condition the air that you breathe. The middle third of the face, where the maxilla and cheekbones sit, is the most important area for both beauty and breathing. Your nasal cavity and your biggest paranasal sinuses, the maxillary sinuses, sit behind your maxilla and cheekbones. The more space they have, the better they can condition air.

After air travels up the nose and through the nasal cavity, it goes down the windpipe (trachea) to the lungs. A forward grown maxilla and mandible leaves lots of room for your windpipe to transport air from the nasal cavity to the lungs. A broad windpipe has no bottlenecks. Recessed jaws cause bottlenecks in your windpipe. The further back the upper and lower jaws are, the tighter the bottlenecks. Beautiful, strong, forward grown jaws signify that we are healthy, and we developed well. We can condition the air that we breathe without becoming compromised and inflamed. Recessed jaws signify that our respiratory system, so fundamental to our survival, is weak.

Bottlenecks make airway inflammation more likely to occur, as the same amount of air (in reality, almost always more air) must go through constricted sections of the windpipe. There, the airway can dry out as it lacks heat and humidity, and become inflamed by dirt.

Recessed jaws make you more likely to suffer from respiratory issues, overbreathing and inflammation due to the smaller nasal cavity and airway.

Look at a face in profile and you can see how forward growth increases nasal cavity size, makes the nose itself look smaller and accommodates a windpipe without bottles necks. It's also objectively more attractive.

The nasal cavity has two meaningful directions of growth, forwards and out to the sides. Facial width and forward growth tend to go together, retaining our potentials. Facial narrowing and recession tend to go together, degrading our potentials.

Airway inflammation is a chronic problem. An inflamed airway becomes smaller in two ways: Firstly, overbreathing causes the airway to constrict when it becomes inflamed from dryness, cold and dirt. Secondly, a layer of mucus forms to protect it, making it smaller still. When we sneeze, blow our noses, or cough, mucus is expelled - sometimes in alarming quantities. These factors are a nightmare for asthma sufferers, because the airways constrict more when breathing in huge quantities of cold, dry, unfiltered air through their mouths, making further breathing much more difficult. Asthma sufferers must deal with chronic dry, dirty, cold airways that constrict due to inflammation, and are made even smaller as mucus is dispersed by the immune system to protect the airway. To compound the issue, people with recessed jaws and squeezed airways are far more likely to suffer from asthma.

To add another layer of complexity, when we mouth breathe, our tongue falls back a little into our throat - causing us to project our head forwards, making our airway smaller still. Mouth breathing affects facial development in the long term, by making the face develop sub-optimally, which impacts beauty potential and long-term breathing as the upper airway is too small. It also affects short-term breathing as the asthma example above highlights, impacting health potential.

The roof of the mouth doesn't drop down when downward growth occurs. The upper teeth and gums drop lower in vertically grown faces - causing a vaulted palate and, sometimes, gummy smiles. Instead, the nasal passages shrink, as low, flat and narrow-set cheekbones, a narrow upper dental arch, and recessed jaws leave too little room.

The nose and nasal passages take up the prime real estate in your face and head. They're so important they're literally front, centre and in the middle of your face. And, unfathomably, many people don't even use their nose. Many today deny their body a low volume of air that is cleaned, temperature-controlled and humidified by the nose and the nasal passages. Instead, they mouth breathe - inhaling unnaturally high volumes of dirty, dry air at the wrong temperature! It's an absolute tragedy of lost health and beauty potentials, inflaming the airway and ruining facial beauty and long-term health.

Breathing & Health

During WWII, Konstantin Buteyko switched his job from engineering to medicine. As a medic, he saw a link between breathing rates and the severity of illness. Most doctors might shrug and say: *They breathe more because they are becoming weaker.* Buteyko, however, stuck to his engineering principles: *If breathing rate increases when someone becomes more sick, and breathing is the variable that we can control, could breath-restriction improve a patient's prognosis?* Or, to put it more simply, is hyperventilation detrimental to everyone?

Buteyko had read about pranayama - the yogic discipline of breathing - and meditation. Tai chi and qigong are two other disciplines that focus on breathing. In his book, *The Oxygen Advantage*, Patrick McKeown quotes a tai chi Master, Chris Pei, who says:

> *"Generally speaking, there are three levels of breathing. The first one is to breathe softly, so that a person standing next to you does not hear your breathing. The second level is to breathe softly so that you do not hear yourself breathing. And the third level is to breathe softly so that you do not feel yourself breathing."[1]*

Overbreathing puts the body is in a continual state of stress and inflammation. When someone falls or jumps into cold water, the body has a conditioned response: The cold shock response. Your mouth opens and you gasp for breath, your blood vessels constrict, your anxiety peaks. Blood flow to your extremities is reduced, so that your vital organs get the lion's share of blood and body heat. The smooth-running of your body is impaired when your body is in a life-or-death struggle.

The body expels its CO_2, which constricts blood flow, in the hopes of minimising heat-loss. In a very cold environment, retaining core temperature is the body's main concern. Quickly expelling CO_2 from your body serves to do this. This stress response increases your chances of getting out alive. It's useful for short-term survival. It's terrible for long-term health. People mimic this stress response every day when they mouth breathe.

Overbreathing alone triggers the body's stress response. It elevates your heart rate, raises your blood pressure, increases your anxiety and adds extra strain to your body. The more you overbreathe, the deeper into your stress response you go.

Overbreathing leads to inflammation of the airway. This, in turn, increases the demand for air, which increases inflammation further. It also decreases the body's tolerance of CO_2. In people who overbreathe, they expel CO_2 at lower blood concentrations because their tolerance for CO_2 is lower, meaning they have to breathe more. Someone with high CO_2 tolerance can wait longer before they expel CO_2 with an exhale. Those with low CO_2 tolerance must exhale sooner as they feel *air hunger* sooner.

Overbreathers have an inflamed airway, inefficient breathing and higher likelihood of developing intolerances to foods or airborne particles. An inflamed airway makes the whole immune system hyper-reactive. This makes autoimmune attacks - where the immune system attacks healthy cells - far more likely.

Quantifying Overbreathing

Modern science suggests that we should have 6-10 breaths per minute. Each breath should be about 500 - 600 millilitres. Breathing volume per minute should be about 5-6 litres. People with breathing inefficiency or respiratory problems can breathe 15 times per minute, with bigger gulps of air. When they breathe a litre of air per breath, they are consuming 15 litres of air per minute.

Let's put the difference between 6 liters and 15 liters[2] into context. Proportionally, it's the same difference as eating 2,500 calories of food a day versus 6,250 calories of food a day. Fifteen litres per minute is so much more air than the respiratory system has evolved to deal with.

No big deal, we may think. Yet it's a huge deal. It's the breathing equivalent of eating 7 or 8 meals per day. When someone chronically hyperventilates, they do so every minute of every day of their lives.

Nostrils are far smaller than an open mouth and can't comfortably labour under that much air. It's easier in inhale 10-15 litres per minute through the mouth than through the nose. Overbreathing in the short term leads to mouth breathing, an airway that dries out and becomes inflamed, less efficient lungs, a lower tolerance to CO_2 levels in the blood, and increased body-wide inflammation.

Overbreathing in the long-term leads to underdeveloped nasal cavities and airways due to recessed jaws, which in turn increases airway inflammation (due to reduced space in the airway), lost beauty potential, an increased risk of intolerances and allergies and destroyed health potential.

Signs of Overbreathing

When you sit near to someone who is breathing loudly, there is a reason that it can be annoying. It's completely unnatural. It's common in the modern world, sure. Yet it's a sign that something wrong with that person. If you have ever felt the desire to walk away from someone who breathes loudly, it's an example of the *Theory of Propinquity*. It's the brain saying, this person comes from an unhealthy environment. The most famous example of this in popular culture - someone to be avoided - is Darth Vader in Star Wars; who's ominous, laboured breathing represents an utterly evil force.

At rest, your breathing should be silent. You may be silent most of the time, yet even people who are mainly silent breathers can overbreathe with a large inhale every few minutes. Here are signs of overbreathing:

- Mouth breathing
- Audible breathing at rest
- Regular sighing
- Making noise when you sit or stand
- Taking big breaths before talking or moving
- Yawning
- The upper chest moving a lot
- Snoring & heavy breathing at night
- Mouth breathing during sleep
- Obvious visible breathing
- Irregular breathing & breath holding

While overbreathing causes mouth breathing, it could also be mouth breathing that causes overbreathing. The nose is a filter and a humidifier of air before it reaches your airway and your lungs. If the airway dries out too much, or it's too dirty, or it's too hot/cold, inflammation occurs and the vicious circle deepens.

It's not just the obvious signs like mouth breathing that you should attune yourself to. When you sit, or stand, or speak, or sigh, you might breathe too much.

Breathing - Virtuous & Vicious Circles

Imagine two friends sitting in a park. One breathes with the Virtuous Circle and the other breathes with the Vicious Circle. They sit in the same air, yet their bodies have very different experiences. The virtuous breather consumes 2.5x less air. Their air is filtered, conditioned, humidified and at a low volume. Vicious breather consumes the exact same air, but it's not filtered, conditioned, humidified or at a low volume. Their airway is inflamed and they likely suffer from allergies or hay fever. The virtuous breather is far more likely to retain their beauty and health potentials than the vicious breather. It's easy to suggest that they are in exactly the same environment. Yet, to their bodies, their environments are drastically different.

The virtuous breathing circle reveals the two active ways to improve breathing efficiency. First, nose breathe exclusively. Second, increase your CO_2 tolerance.

Nose breathing is the only natural way to breathe.

Overbreathing & Inflammation

What Inflames The Airway?

- Air that is too hot/cold
- Air that is too dry
- Irritants in the airway (from unfiltered air)
- Too much air

The Case For Carbon Dioxide

Carbon dioxide has long been seen as a waste product in the body, like exhaust gases in internal combustion engines. However, in reality, CO_2 is important to the functioning of the body. It helps transfer oxygen from the blood into a cell. It helps blood vessels to relax. It helps keep our blood pH levels stable.

CO_2 is not simply a waste gas. It is vital to proper circulation and full-body health. As Yandell Henderson said *"Carbon Dioxide is, in fact, a more fundamental component of living matter than is Oxygen."*[3]

How Carbon Dioxide plays such a large role is key to understanding why overbreathing - expelling too much CO_2 with each and every breath - leads to long-lasting problems in the body.

Oxygen Transfer

You need 5% CO_2 in the blood to release the oxygen to each cell. This process, called the *Bohr Effect,* decreases the bind of oxygen to haemoglobin when the blood carries enough CO_2. If the levels of CO_2 are lower than 5%, oxygen isn't optimally released into the cells. Tissues and organs with lower levels of oxygen can't perform optimally. Overbreathe, and your cells aren't getting all the oxygen they need, as CO_2 levels fall below 5%.

Overbreathing doesn't improve oxygen levels in your body. It does the opposite. You reduce oxygen delivery because you exhale too much CO_2 for there to be 5% in the blood. This is the paradox of breathing; overbreathing leads to less oxygen in your tissue and organs. It leads to poor circulation for two reasons. One: Oxygen doesn't get to every cell efficiently because of the Bohr Effect. Two: During a stress response, blood vessels in the extremities constrict, and blood is redirected to your core organs.

CO_2 Tolerance

The medulla oblongata is a cone-shaped part of your brain stem, which dictates your tolerance for CO_2. It controls breathing. Conventional wisdom would suggest that we breathe our next breath because our body needs more oxygen. Surprisingly, this isn't the trigger for the medulla. CO_2's level in the blood is the trigger. We can live for 3 minutes without oxygen, yet our CO_2 tolerance defines how long we can comfortably leave between each breath - how long we can not breathe until we feel *air hunger.*

The tolerance that the medulla oblongata sets is changeable. Expose it to more CO_2, and it will adapt to cope with more CO_2 before triggering air hunger. Expose it to less, through chronic overbreathing, and it will demand the next breath sooner.

The medulla oblongata's tolerance to CO_2 is an important metric to overall health. Low tolerance to CO_2 leads to a feeling of suffocation (air hunger), which increases breathing volume. Having a higher tolerance to CO_2 reduces our breathing volume and improves our efficiency. When someone can cope with 6% CO_2 in the blood, every cell gets all the oxygen transfer it needs, they breathe lightly and calmly, and the immune system can rest.

CO_2 And You

CO_2 level in the atmosphere is around 0.04%. It's crept up due to man-made emissions - to about 400 parts per million. Its natural level is 0.035% - 350 parts per million. Optimal CO_2 levels in your lungs are around 7%. That's 175 times more than it is in air - 70,000 parts per million.

Oxygen levels in the atmosphere are around 21%. We exhale approximately 75% of the O_2 that we inhale at rest and about 20% during strenuous exercise.

We need to produce far more CO_2 than exists in the air and we use less O_2 than is in the air. We should stop seeing ourselves as an O_2 factory. We should begin to see ourselves as a CO_2 factory. Our aim should be to produce and maintain high levels of CO_2 through physical exercise and breathing exercises to increase CO_2 tolerance. When we breathe lightly, we maintain higher CO_2 levels.

What Decreases CO_2 Tolerance?

- Overbreathing
- Mouth Breathing
- Food Intolerance & Allergies
- Being Overweight
- Low Fitness Levels
- Small airway / lack of forward growth.
- Low Vitamin D
- Heated Bedrooms

When you allow your breathing to become punctuated by large sighs and big breaths, you expel carbon dioxide and gradually reduce the body's tolerance to it. Overbreathing is very common and unnatural. You should continually work to become more efficient with air.

Buteyko Breathing - Light Is Right

Dr Buteyko discovered that lighter breathing was beneficial to asthma sufferers. Some dispute the explanation that Buteyko practitioners give. However, the more efficient you are with air, the healthier your respiratory system will be. It's designed to naturally expect about 5 litres per minute. Problems occur when you creep over that. The extent of the problems occurring mirrors the extent of overbreathing. It's a dial, not a switch.

Aiming for *air efficiency* and reducing airway inflammation can slowly but surely reset our breathing rates and - when used in conjunction with an anti-inflammatory diet - our total body immune response.

Exercise Is The Natural CO_2 Tolerance Builder

When you exercise and move your body, the body creates more CO_2 than when at rest. The harder/longer you exercise, the more CO_2 is released.

Sustained exercise causes the body to become more tolerant to CO_2. This is because the body adapts to higher CO_2. Exercise isn't just good because your muscles get stronger. It creates a healthier, more efficient respiratory system. When you increase CO_2 tolerance, you reduce breathing volume. Your immune system dials down its "threat level" - it's state of arousal - because there are dramatically fewer threats when nose breathing and low breathing volume are combined.

The other way to increase CO_2 tolerance is through breathing exercises.

Breathing And Me

It first struck me when I learned scuba diving. On dives, you buddy up. Two people go down together - buddies - and rise when one of them is low on air. I was paired with short, Irish girl. After seeing a host of tropical sea-life, I realised my air supply was very low. I swam over and showed her, signalling that we need to go to the surface. She shrugged underwater, as if to say, *"How?!"* Her supply was over half full.

I have never been asthmatic. I thought that efficiency of breathing is binary; either you're asthmatic or you're fine. Yet, that incident was my first clue that I was highly inefficient with air. At the time, I believed it was due to our height difference. Only later, when I fully considered that breathing efficiency occurs on a spectrum, I remembered the scuba diving story and that my breathing was inefficient.

My body was inflamed for as long as I can remember. Generally, for me, this surfaced as eczema. My chronic eczema disappeared only when I removed all inflammatory foods from my diet, and when I used a breathing device which trained my body to be much more efficient with air.

Health Quadrant II: What to Eat (Further Reading)

The Gut

Recap: There are four immune systems in the body. The largest is the gut.

Our gastrointestinal tract - gut or G.I. tract - is where our health is largely defined. The gut wall is vital for absorbing nutrients the body needs and for keeping harmful particles out of the bloodstream. Food of no value is usually excreted as waste, or it breaches the gut wall.

Your gut goes on the offensive when it senses food which it believes is dangerous. Gut health is vital to overall health, as the gut is the biggest part of the immune system in your body. When your gut isn't healthy, your immune system will be compromised.

In a healthy gut, only the good stuff - vitamins, minerals, amino acids, natural sugars and digested foods - pass through. In an unhealthy gut, the immune system goes into overdrive. When the gut wall is compromised, waste or under-digested foods can crash through holes in the gut into the bloodstream. At this point, white blood cells hunt down invaders wherever they are in the body. This causes collateral damage anywhere that blood flows, which is virtually everywhere.

The gut wall produces mucus to protect it from harmful particles breaking through. But it's vulnerable to being broken through, as it's just one cell thick. That one-cell barrier and a tiny film of mucus are all we have to stop the march of harmful particles reaching our bloodstream and causing issues in virtually every organ.

Lectins – such as gluten - at the scale of gut wall thickness, are big, sticky proteins which bind to mucosal sugars on the gut wall. If your mucus has been disrupted (due to eating lectins already) the lectin will stick directly to the wall. It will then produce a protein called zonulin which breaks apart the mucus lining. Then, lectins flood through these holes in your gut wall. Then, lots of the harmful waste particles that should be excreted pass into the bloodstream. These particles sneaking through your gut wall cause leaky gut.

When your gut is compromised, it's as if your castle walls have been breached. A whole host of hostile bacteria, which have no business being in your blood, attack. One is called lipopolysaccharides (LPS) which the immune system attacks constantly when it breaches the gut wall. LPS bacteria reach *all* your body's cells. This constant attack of these cells can cause collateral damage in places which seemingly never relate to what you ate, such as your brain, your joints, or your eyes.

The body deals with these invasions by activating our white blood cells. They converge around the holes in our gut wall. These white blood cell foot soldiers need fuel. As a temporary measure, to fuel the white blood cells, the body stores visceral fat next to your gut. This gives them a constant local energy supply. Visceral fat - fat stored in the abdominal cavity, near the liver, stomach and intestines - is the most deadly fat in the body. It disrupts hormones and organs, and causes long-term damage when it persists. For modern people, our gut walls are constantly being breached and visceral fat exists permanently.

Visceral fat is implicated in chronic conditions such as diabetes, heart disease, heart attacks, high blood pressure, strokes, cancers and Alzheimer's disease. Another cause of visceral fat is from a fatty liver, caused by having high blood sugar. The most dangerous of these sugars is fructose, which also interferes with protective proteins and mucus in the gut.

Imagine your job is to protect a gut. And every meal, you're filled with wave after wave of gut-piercing particles and bloodstream invaders. You must defend. The first time, you may be taken by surprise. However, on a long enough timeline, your attacks become more violent. You turn into a grizzled veteran whose policy is, "Attack first, think later." As the harmful particles breach your gut wall and infiltrate everywhere - muscles, joints, brain, thyroid, nerves, skin - you shoot them down and also hit the surrounding tissues. The accrued damage from "friendly fire" on your healthy cells eventually leads to chronic conditions.

Have poor skin? Your gut wall is breached. Chronic headaches? Your gut wall is breached. Nerve problems? You guessed it, your gut wall is breached. White blood cells cause collateral damage in any part of the body where enemy particles are found. They are trigger-happy soldiers with a bad aim.

By continuing to eat foods which punch through the gut, you continue to allow a war to wage throughout your body. When your gut can't heal those tiny holes, lectins and other problematic invaders continually sneak through, leaving your body an inflamed war zone.

Inflammation is a good thing when you cut your hand or sprain your ankle. It helps you to recover. However, chronic inflammation - where the body repeatedly attacks itself - is terrible for your health and development. Recovery is impossible when an attack is sustained, meal after meal, day after day.

An overactive immune system triggered by a leaky gut causes constant inflammation.

Importantly, this inflammation affects *breathing* in two ways:

1, Your body is put in a stress response, increasing breathing volume.

2, White blood cells target invaders in the blood in your lungs and airway, causing collateral damage to friendly cells.

The Dial of Inflammation

Inflammation occurs on a spectrum. It's a dial, not a switch. The dial is how some people can have very mild, localized psoriasis, yet others are affected everywhere. Health foods are simply the foods which make *you* healthy. They may be different to foods which make other people healthy. The key is knowing what your body responds best and worst to. Removing dairy, grains, sugar and sugar substitutes is the best starting point to discover what upsets your body as these are the usual suspects.

Lectins, allergens, salicylates, histamine foods, oxalates and more can affect some people in ways that they don't affect others. The only thing that matters is what applies to you. You may respond poorly to gluten or other lectins. Others may have issues with foods high in salicylates. For others still, it's dairy. In this way, we are all unique.

Most Western people tend to eat three meals, spread out through the day. Each meal tends to contain lots of ingredients. Inflammation responses can take three days from a food's consumption to occur. That means that it could be any ingredient(s) from 9 meals, plus snacks or drinks, that cause inflammation.

Sherlock Holmes would struggle to figure out what the specific trigger is, if you become inflamed. For this reason, anyone who has autoimmune problems should get blood tested, or embark on an elimination diet to discover their triggers.

Autoimmunity Leads to Chronic Inflammation

As we have seen, an overactive immune system attacks good cells which are close to immune system insults. The possible results of autoimmunity (the process where the immune system attacks healthy cells) includes joint pain, weight gain, gut issues, brain fog, depression, mood disorders and fatigue. The common reasons given for these symptoms are ageing or stress. The accumulation of damage caused by the body attacking itself is noticeable, then painful, then irreversible.

Medics typically run tests and find nothing, when you begin to feel bad. Everything looks normal to them because their tests seek out *crises*. Medics advise, in those instances, to get better sleep, remove stress and lose weight, typically. They can't *see* the problem.

Your body, however, is giving you clues that you are on the path to autoimmune diseases. You can feel the affects of autoimmunity without ever being diagnosed with a disease. Doctors can only diagnose something after significant tissue damage occurs. This tissue damage can surface in any cell in your body, through a constant attack on your healthy cells by an overactive immune system. Yet if there is micro-damage across your body, no tissue damage will be seen in those tests.

Let's say you never eat added sugar, and your blood sugar is stable. Once a year, you eat an Easter egg. You will not go through the stages that lead to diabetes. You won't have sugar cravings, hypoglycaemia, metabolic syndrome, weight gain, numbness and tingling, then be told you have diabetes and a higher risk of heart disease. Progression towards autoimmune diseases occurs through repeated exposure to triggers that cause autoimmune attacks on your body. Eat chocolate every day of the year, and those symptoms may appear.

Asthma is an autoimmune disease. The triggers could be airborne insults, foods or both. When your gut wall is compromised and you overbreathe, asthma can take over. The correct response to asthma is improving your breathing efficiency and discovering and eliminating food triggers. Failure to do so will cause symptoms to remain, or to get worse. Breathing can spiral into a vicious circle.

Science has emerged that heart disease and even cancer may be the results of chronic inflammation. The immune system is the only thing that can cause inflammation in the body. Triggers to the immune system are therefore implicated in the top three causes of death - heart disease, cancer and autoimmune diseases. Discovering your immune system triggers through this lens becomes a matter of your long-term health. And to be clear, bread will be a trigger for some. For others it will be the lectins in tomatoes. For others still it will be the salicylates in spinach. "Healthy foods" dietary advice is useless to you, if you have an autoimmune response to the foods they claim are healthy! It's akin to someone saying peanuts are healthy when you have a nut allergy.

Be aware of both pressure and time. Stop the pressure by eating and breathing in ways that relax your immune system. To maintain a diet that reduces inflammation is a lifelong commitment.

Inflammatory Foods - The Big Three

From the 1950s, there has been a war on dietary fat. The belief that animal fats cause heart disease - led by belligerent physiologist Ancel Keys - caused a huge restructuring of diets.

The food pyramid is a carb-heavy, low-fat set of guidelines. The base of the pyramid is made up of breads, cereals, pasta and rice. Grains and sugar have won the war of the dinner plate. There was a problem with most foods being fat-free. Protein is not nearly as tasty as fat. You simply have to compare an egg white (containing virtually no fat), with an egg yolk (nearly 60% fat) to understand that most natural flavour comes from fat.

Removing fat caused loss of flavour. This is where refined sugar came in. Mountains of sugar have been pumped into food.

Grains

The shift in modern times from unprocessed foods to processed foods wreaks havoc on beauty and health potentials. Take bread. No human being sees wheat growing in a field and thinks that eating a wheat kernel is delicious. It's a food we cultivated - very recently, in evolutionary terms. It requires lots of processing to become appetising. And gluten causes gut permeability for everyone. Yes, everyone.

Gluten, *"induces an increase in intestinal permeability in all individuals[.]"*[1] It tears up everyone's gut. No human being has evolved all the enzymes to fully digest grain proteins. For some people this is not a big deal, as their immune systems ignore it. For others, it begins a huge cascade of health declines which we wrongly attribute to ageing.

Make no mistake: Bread is one of the best foods for feeding large populations. Yet, on an individual level, it can be deeply problematic.

Sugar

Sugar is very rare in nature. Fresh fruits provide sugar. Honey provides sugar. Yet, in natural terms, these items are often out-of-season. Sugar's benefit is its taste. In all other ways, it's bad for you. *"Fructose can... disrupt gut barrier integrity, resulting in systemic endotoxemia, leading to the activation of an inflammatory cascade"*[2] like asthma, hay fever, or any chronic inflammatory problem that affects so many people today.

A 2011 study found that diabetics had worse lung function (and pulmonary function) than their non-diabetic peers. Sugar is heavily correlated with diabetes. What you eat - or more accurately, how your body deals with food - has huge implications on every aspect of facial development and overall health.

Dairy

The prevalence of lactose intolerance internationally is 68%.[3] This is primarily because cow's milk is designed for calves. We have not only relied on dairy for butter, cheese, milk and cream, we have also pasteurised it and filtered it. Many people who consume too much dairy are at risk of inflammation.

Not All Veg Is Good for All People

As the last Ice Age hit, many plants that humans had relied on for millennia became extinct. Our ancestors, in their quest for survival, cultivated new crops. Most of the vegetables we eat today are from a few common ancestors. It's easy to believe that bell peppers and chillies are from the same family. It's harder to believe that tomatoes and potatoes share a common ancestor. In fact, all four share the *same* common ancestor and are part of the nightshade family. Other nightshade plants include tobacco, eggplants, goji berries and blueberries. They are all very high in lectins, and all originate from the Americas. Most European, Asian and African peoples weren't exposed to these foods until a few hundred years ago.

Animals have very good immediate defences against death. They can attack, run away or stay completely still to avoid being eaten. They have claws, teeth, horns, size, strength and speed. The fight, flight or freeze response is an animal's survival instinct in action. Plants, on the other hand, have no option to bite us, run away or to try to hide themselves. Plants want to survive and replicate just like animals do.

Nature's solution for plants includes immediate defences - poison, paralysis or traps for their predators; or long-term defences - slowly causing sickness amongst animals who eat them.

The Dangers in Plant Foods

- Lectins
- Wheat Germ Agglutinin
- Salicylates
- Oxalates
- Nightshades

- Amines
- Histamines
- Glutamates
- Sulphites/Thiols

These plant defences can cause problems if we have gut permeability, and our immune system reacts to them. When those two events occur, a whole host of subtle negative consequences can take place. However, for many people, plants cause no inflammatory cascade.

Meat Is Inflammation-Free

Animal defences emerge before they are killed, not after they are eaten. Meat has a balance of amino acids that almost exactly correlates with human requirements for essential amino acids. It's nutrient-dense, tough to break off and chew, and it doesn't cause inflammation in people who suffer from autoimmune conditions.

In Western studies on health, meat is shown to be unhealthy. In Eastern societies there is no association between meat consumption and mortality. These studies rely on self-reporting. In the West, people who eat meat are more likely to live unhealthily, due to the narrative around saturated fats. In Asia, there was never an attack on fat. Meat-eating was aspirational and evidence of it being bad for health is slim.

What to Eat & Me

I took a test to see what caused inflammation in my body. I learned I was allergic to wild grass. Yet, the most interesting findings were to do with food. I was intolerant to virtually everything that I was fed as a child. Tomatoes, wheat, dairy, mushrooms, yeast, chillies, peanuts, sugars and sweeteners.

This is not uncommon for people who are chronically inflamed. I recommend that everyone gets tested. My website lists the best tests to use.

In my 30s I had a huge eczema outbreak and took drastic action. I started doing breathing exercises and using the breathing device that reset breathing rate. I went on a full, week-long, water only fast. Then I began eating a carnivore diet, the furthest from my childhood diet, and free of inflammatory properties.

Within a month, the eczema that had plagued me for life disappeared. This was while cutting all moisturiser use. I reset my breathing, my gut and what I ate. This new diet facilitated *how to eat* more naturally. I felt better than I had felt in years. My body, for the first time I could remember, was not inflamed.

Health Quadrant II (Continued): When To Eat (Further Reading)

Eating Frequency

Western countries place food as a central part of culture, family and society. Food is also big business. Yet, "three meals a day" is a social construct. In the 1920s and 1930s the British government promoted breakfast as the most important meal of the day. This coincided with the emergence of breakfast cereals, which provided cheap, long-lasting, convenient food that was ready-to-eat. The famous snippet of advice, that breakfast is "*the most important meal of the day*" emerged from a 1944 U.S. advertising campaign by General Foods. In American grocery stores, pamphlets were handed out, promoting the value of breakfast. Radios everywhere broadcast the following: "*Nutrition experts say breakfast is the most important meal of the day.*" And so, it became the received wisdom of the post-war Western world.

This constant barrage of the message has spanned the globe. I still hear it spouted today. American breakfasts - before cereal - consisted of eggs, pastries and pancakes. Meat was also served. Cereals - the highly processed and highly sugared food that reigns today - ascended to dominance due to aggressive marketing and convenience for people who were in a morning rush to work or school.

Breakfast was never a big meal before advertising dollars promoted it as such. It wasn't a part of everyone's morning routine. When I was a boy, I'd wake up, grab a bowl, pour in breakfast cereal - the sweeter and more chocolaty, the better! - and then carefully try to pour milk over every grain in the bowl. That was the beginning of my day, every day. Yet, before we'd been sold the idea that breakfast is vital, and cereal is the best form that breakfast can take, many cultures and societies didn't eat it at all.

The Romans only ate once, at around noon. They believed - science and this author might agree - that this was healthier than repeated meals each day. As food historian Caroline Yeldham has said, "*The Romans believed it was healthier to eat only one meal a day. They were obsessed with digestion and eating more than one meal was considered a form of gluttony.*"[1]

In medieval Europe, there is debate about whether breakfast was skipped, or a luxury for the wealthy, or only for laborers. Breakfast was a privilege for a wealthy few, or a necessity for a very active group of labourers, depending on who you ask and where you look. Most people, it seems, went without breakfast. Europe survived on two meals per day. American colonists ate breakfast, but only after morning work.

Breakfast became a first thing-in-the-morning ritual when we moved to cities. People were due in places at set times - be it factories, shops or offices. As people left the home all day, breakfast rose to prominence. First they ate meat, bread and eggs. Later, cereals were invented.

This three-meal culture is a product of industrialization and advertising. The addition of sugar in cereals led to the Kellogg brothers falling out and forming separate companies. Unsurprisingly, the brother who condoned adding sugar to cereal - he had described cereal without sugar as *"horse-food"*[2] - became the Kellogg's brand that we know today.

It takes a lot of advertising dollars to make societies change their eating culture permanently. For cereals to really dominate, it took a bland grain, coated in a glaze of sugar and filled with colors and flavourings, then fortified with vitamins to trick parents into believing that these dangerously addictive bowls of empty nutrition were healthy. And children were aggressively targeted. Everyone knows Tony the Tiger, and the Snap, Crackle & Pop of Rice Krispies. We also know, of course, how little chewing is required after they are soaked in milk. Heavy marketing meant that kids would eat the same meal every day, for years. It also reinforced the relatively new idea that eating first thing in the morning was normal.

As Abigail Carroll suggests in her book Three Squares: The Invention of the American Meal:[3]

> *Eating three meals a day was basically invented due to culture. When European settlers got to America, they found Native Americans were basically just eating whenever they felt the urge to, rather than at specified times.*

Eating three meals a day for our ancestors was a near impossibility. There is no biological imperative to eat three times daily. People appear to have eaten, much like animals, when they could get food.

Employment seems to be the reason that breakfast became common-place. It is only in the last 500 years or so that people have been employed in the sense that we understand it. A tenant who worked his

Lord's land would do so when it fit around his schedule. The modern timetable of work seems to have emerged in Britain in the 16th Century. A statute in 1515 declared that from mid-March to mid-September, the working day of craftsmen and labourers should start at 5am, and end at 7-8pm, with 90 minutes for dinner. People who worked for a living, rather than living off the land, shaped the modern three meals a day.

Natural Eating

Breakfast may be a cultural norm that came into being because of work timetables and standardized time. However, why is eating frequency significant?

Naturally, we are built to go without food for a day or more. This is a perfectly normal part of being a hunter or forager in the wild.

What we eat plays a very clear role in how hungry we are. It's worth noting that natural, unprocessed foods are better for satiating our appetites than processed grain and high-sugar foods.

Indeed, when we go for long periods without food, the body diverts energy that would usually be used for digesting to other pursuits. When we go without food, our human Growth Hormone (hGH) levels spike. This is probably because in nature, to get enough food, we had to exert ourselves physically. Going longer without food means that the body speeds up adaptation. This is an evolved response. If you are engaging in an activity a lot, say running, it pays to dramatically increase hGH, so that you become stronger and faster to catch prey, for example.

hGH also preserves muscle. This means the body takes most of its energy from stored body fat. Fasting for 3 days increases hGH by 300%. When someone fasts for a week, their hGH levels increase by 1,250%.[4] Eating prompts growth hormone levels to drop back to normal. When we think of jaw muscles, there is a clear benefit to having higher hGH levels when we chew. Our jaws develop faster and with more strength, enhancing our beauty potential in so doing.

Growth hormones aren't the only - or even the main - benefit of extended periods without food. There is something even more transformative...

Autophagy

In Stockholm City Hall, on 10 December 2016, a man was awarded the world's most prestigious prize for his research into simple baker's yeast by His Majesty the King of Sweden. Yoshinori Ohsumi won a Nobel Prize, in the category of Physiology or Medicine, after proving that cells in the body recycle their components to enhance their function and adapt to changing circumstances. This self-cleansing is called autophagy.

Ohsumi not only verified that autophagy occurs, he also identified the genes that allow the process to take place. He discovered that all nucleated cells are capable of autophagy. This means that every cell can remove the weakest elements of its structure and replace or rebuild them to increase the health of that cell. Autophagy begins to occur when we move into a fasted state. This replenishing of cells is integral to health. Indeed, when the regulation of autophagy is impaired, serious human diseases proliferate; cancer, infections, diabetes and debilitating nervous system issues.

The constant cycle of three daily meals, punctuated by snacks between meals, means that for many of us, autophagy is never reached. Autophagy is vital for keeping the body as healthy as possible at a cellular level. Lots of meals and snacks are the great disruptor of this process.

Autophagy kicks into gear after around 18-20 hours of fasting. This can be sped up through exercise. After 36 hours without food, autophagy increases by 300%. At this point, the body's cells start a deep clean. After 48 hours autophagy goes up by another 30%. It peaks at the 72-hour stage. It is said that peak healing occurs in a fasted state. This is because autophagy flourishes in a fasted body.

We understand that those who are very ill - animals or humans - reject food and water. When an animal is injured and goes somewhere quiet to try to recuperate, they enter a fasted state. Pets who are injured typically refuse food.

Fasting, Autophagy & Fat Loss

Food isn't the only energy source for our bodies. Another source of energy to sustain us that many people hate, but also struggle to get rid of is body fat.

Fat is a rich reserve of energy that exists in anticipation of food scarcity. Upon fasting, fat is burned for energy. This is one of the most natural survival strategies we have. The only reason we store excessive body fat is to burn it during lean times in the future. Unfortunately, our evolution hasn't caught up with our modern eating habits. We can eat day and night without expending energy. Fat, for many of us, is never burned as the lean times never come.

Fat is an insurance policy - like any insurance policy - against a future disastrous event. In the case of our body, it's insurance against a famine situation. The issue with insurance policies is that they are always liabilities until the moment they are required. Storing fat long-term is a huge liability to your health.

Fasting Benefits

There are intermittent fasting protocols which I recommend. My reasons for supporting intermittent fasting protocols for better facial development include:

- Improved breathing efficiency & mouth posture
- Increased human growth hormone for facial musculature & for bone remodelling
- Healthier gut microbiome
- Lower incidence of inflammation
- Autophagy

The astounding fact that you can increase Human Growth Hormone by over 1,000% means that people can chew hard gum before they eat, and their jaw muscles will grow more quickly. People who go to the gym can optimize their regime by working out in a fasted state. After the workout they can eat for the best recovery.

List of benefits:

- Weight Loss
- Inflammation Reduction
- Lower Insulin Levels (& Diabetes Risk)
- Improved Heart Health
- Lower risk of cancer
- Improved Brain health
- Extended Lifespan

Health Quadrant III: Exercise

Exercise & Humanity

Human beings were never the strongest, the fastest, or had the most protective armour. Instead, we had guile. In our vast hunter-gatherer past - which represents 95% of *homo sapiens* history and 99.9% of all human (*homo*) history - we were very active. We moved with the seasons, hunted, and foraged. This gave us strength, endurance, agility and flexibility. Our Beauty Quadrant & Health Quadrant were fulfilled by living this way. The natural movements that hunters engage in were diverse and functional. Animals don't sweat as effectively as man. We ran over varied terrain until an animal was exhausted. Then we would throw something heavy or sharp at it, approach it and kill it, then carve it up and carry large sections to a campfire. Even building a fire requires collecting wood or felling small trees, carrying that fuel, then creating a fire. All of this requires movement, endurance, strength and energy.

When agriculture spread between 10,000-12,000 years ago, human heights dropped dramatically. Diets, which had once been more meat-heavy and varied, became far less varied, consisting of one or two grains, and lacked all the nutrients and essential amino acids that humans require to reach our height and health potentials. To catch animals we must run, looking forwards. To grow food, we need to bend down and tend to plants. Exercise, posture, and complete nutrition were compromised by our transition to farming.

These days, most of us sit inside, in offices, looking at screens. We drive to work. We sit at home, at work and on our journeys to each. Our exercise levels have plummeted. We evolved to be hunter gatherers and we have become sedentary animals who retain our hunter gatherer limbs and environmental expectations. These expectations are not being met.

Exercise & Breathing

Exercise is an environmental expectation. It can help with breathing when you breathe nasally during exercise. The best way to do this is to do the exercises in the *Breathing Exercises (Part Two)* section of this book. Exercise has been repeatedly shown to improve breathing efficiency and reduce demand for air.

Exercise & Posture

Natural posture occurs when your muscles are all well developed, naturally holding the body upright at rest. This is in part due to how you choose to stand and sit, and in part due to how your muscles hold your form.

Yoga is proven to improve both posture and breathing. The increase in muscle strength, flexibility and respiratory function contributing to more natural posture. I list the best yoga practitioners for online classes at tcarneybowles.com/yoga

Exercise & Immunity

Exercise helps with breathing and posture. It also helps the immune system, further fortifying the Health Quadrant. We have less need for immune support when we breathe efficiently and are fit and strong - and a stronger immune system when immune support is required. Exercise provokes a virtuous circle of protection for the Health Quadrant.

Body Fat & Beauty

There are two ways in which beauty potential is corroded. Our facial bones may develop sub optimally. Or facial and body fat may disguise beauty. Exercise and what we eat impact our levels of body fat.

Overweight people have large masses of visceral fat around their mid-section. The immune system tries to fight and nullify the invaders that break through the gut wall. The fat that forms in this area is fuel for white blood cells to hunt down insults that escape the gut.

Visceral fat puts the body in a constant state of inflammation. It's intended as a temporary measure. However, eating foods that insult the immune system and break through the gut wall constantly leads to long-term visceral fat. Exercise and diet changes are the only ways to effectively get rid of this fat.

Being a healthy body weight improves looks, health and cognitive function. Indeed, diet or exercise in isolation improve those three potentials. Combine diet and exercise, and you have a potent potential-maximising weapon against declines in beauty, health and brain power.

Exercise & Me

I have always been relatively fit but never extremely so. I was reasonable at cross-country running at school. But I was keeled over at the end, having mouth-breathed throughout each race.

Health Quadrant IV: Vitamin D (Further Reading)

Vitamin D Blood Levels

Less than 20 ng/ml	Deficient
20-29 ng/ml	Insufficient
30-39 ng/ml	Sufficient
40-59 ng/ml	Safe
60-89 ng/ml	Optimal
Greater than 150 ng/ml	Toxic

Figure 53 - Vitamin D levels in the blood.

Why Vitamin D Is Part of The Health Quadrant

Vitamin D reduces inflammation. It plays a role in maintaining good health in most areas of the body; most importantly for growth, airway inflammation and protecting against insults to the immune system. It's not strictly a vitamin, but a secosteroid. When Vitamin D levels go down, inflammation-risk goes up. Most people who live in modern societies are dangerously low in Vitamin D and dangerously high in chronic inflammation. While Vitamin D deficiency is common, it is not natural.

Modern life keeps us indoors, away from the most abundant source of Vitamin D; the sun. Modern medicine seems far more concerned with Vitamin D toxicity (where we have far too much) than with Vitamin D deficiency. Yet, Vitamin D toxicity is extremely rare, and Vitamin D deficiency is extremely common.

Vitamin D maintains a strong Health Quadrant.

Vitamin D Testing

Vitamin D levels are measured through a blood test. (See *Figure 41* for the ranges.) Everyone who wants optimal health should get tested to see if they are Vitamin D deficient.

Our best estimates for optimal levels of Vitamin D are based testing nomadic hunter-gatherer tribes around the world. The levels of 25(OH) D in each millilitre of blood reveals how much Vitamin D is in the body.

Vitamin D Deficiency

The recommended daily dose for Vitamin D was 200 IU (International Units) before 1997. Now, it stands at 400-600 IU.[1] This is a still drastically low number, designed only to get people out of the deficient range.

100 IU per day increases vitamin D blood levels 1 ng/ml. 400 IU per day increases vitamin D blood levels 4 ng/ml. 1,000 IU per day increases vitamin D blood levels 10 ng/ml. 2,000 IU per day increases vitamin D blood levels 20 ng/ml. Vitamin D takes months to build up. When you take 2,000 IU a day, you don't immediately jump by 20 ng/ml.

When indigenous people work and live outside, their levels of Vitamin D are between the 40-60 ng/ml levels at least. This reveals the natural, optimal range for people.

In Northern Europe, 92% of the population have levels lower than 20 ng/ml. In the USA, it's 36%. In Australia, 31%. In Canada, 61%. In India, 75%. This isn't a *slightly* lower level than you should have. This is the absolute lowest range. Rickets can occur with 14 ng/ml in the blood. Having anything under 20 ng/ml should terrify most people. Yet, it is very common throughout modern humanity.

Even in sunny places, Vitamin D deficiency is common. In Miami, which has sunshine for 249 days a year, 39% of the adult population are Vitamin D deficient. Australian Dermatologists? 83% are Vitamin D deficient.[2] And not just 20 ng/ml, but below 16 ng/ml. 15% of those had less than 7 ng/ml.[3]

Natural Levels of Vitamin D Throughout History

Before agriculture, we would go where the food was, where the water was, where the best weather was. And weather is our focus right now. We've evolved to live outside like every other animal.

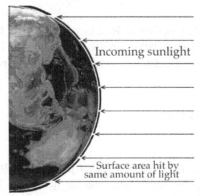

Figure 54 – How the same quantity of sunlight covers a larger area the further you are from the equator.

As people spread across the planet, and branched into the northern hemisphere, evolutionary adaptation lowered the levels of melanin in the skin. Some humans became whiter, as the intensity of the sun is lower at latitudes further from the equator. (See *Figure 54.*) Vitamin D is more easily produced for lighter-skinned people. The need to protect the skin under the intense equatorial sun caused dark skin. The need to produce enough Vitamin D further from the equator led to lighter skin groups emerging.

This shows us the paramount importance of producing enough Vitamin D. Vitamin D's benefits to stave off inflammation has transformed human skin tones throughout the world. Every human being on earth comes from black ancestry. The only reason many people aren't black today is because of the need to produce Vitamin D more efficiently in areas with weaker sunlight.

Our differing skin tones, and each individual's response to sunshine, can be explained by thinking about the types of habitable land on our planet. Strength of sunlight is one factor. The type of land indigenous people lived on is another.

Habitable Land on Planet Earth

Of the habitable land on planet earth 10,000 years ago, 57% was forests and 42% was grassland and shrubs. The final 1% was lakes and rivers. We evolved in forests and grassland. Grassland inhabitants are both more exposed and often closer to the equator. Grasslands are drier, generally warmer and have less cloud cover than forests. People from those places have darker skin.

European countries were covered, for most of their history, by vast, thick forests. The canopy of trees doesn't block out all sunlight. Sunshine peaks through. This is what white skinned people evolved to expect; beams of weaker, high-latitude sunlight, peaking through the trees onto the skin. The requirement for sunshine is greater in dark skinned people, who typically lived under high intensity sunshine on grasslands.

The amount of sunshine needed by those who live in forests and those who live on grasslands are different, even at the same latitude. The balance between Vitamin D production and protection from the sun is very different for an equatorial grassland inhabitant than for a high-latitude forest dweller, and this is reflected in skin tone. Vitamin D production is such an important aspect of living healthily that some of us are very pale skinned and others are very dark skinned.

Sunburn & Skin Cancer

The danger of skin cancer - and skin damage from sunshine - shouldn't be understated. You should protect yourself from burning at all costs. People who live far from where their ancestors evolved - European-skinned people in Australia or Asian-skinned people in Africa - must be more careful with sunshine exposure. Don't burn!

Applying sun cream every time you are in the sun can cause you to burn, if you ever forget to apply it. Lack of sun exposure causes skin to become paler. A body starved of sunlight adapts to be incredibly responsive to it. The sun-deprived body takes in every meagre beam of sunlight to covert to Vitamin D. When a body adapts to a world where sunlight seems rare due to sun cream, strong sunlight becomes dangerous, and sunburn becomes likely.

Having lots of Vitamin D reduces the risk of sunburn. Take supplements and limit your daily sunshine (without sun cream) to 30 minutes per day to increase your Vitamin D levels.

When I first supplemented high doses of Vitamin D, I worked outside for a weekend in the summer. Usually, I would burn. But I didn't. Colleagues who had naturally darker skin burned. Vitamin D, the inflammation-killer, is produced by sunshine, and it also can protect us from sun burn.

Is Sunscreen Good?

SPF of 30 absorbs 95%-98% of solar UBV radiation. Let's call it 97% for this example. Now, imagine someone forgets to apply sunscreen one time. Their percentage increase of UBV radiation is 3,233% more than they have adapted to deal with. This is a remarkable increase and the increase itself can lead to skin damage. Once you have received a healthy 15-30 minutes of daily sunshine, apply sun cream. If you worry about face wrinkles, always wear sun cream on your face. If your skin gets pink before 30 minutes of sun exposure, move out of the sun, or wear sunscreen.

Autoimmune Diseases

Being born at, or living near, the equator has been repeatedly found to reduce the risk of autoimmune diseases. There is mounting evidence that illness itself is just chronic inflammation. Optimal Vitamin D3 levels negates inflammation and autoimmune diseases. Multiple sclerosis increases by 100% if you were born at a latitude of 40 degrees North compared with 33 degrees North. Type 1 diabetes follows a U-shaped curve, where the incidents of diabetes are higher the further North or South of the equator you are.

The Finnish were worried about Vitamin D levels, so they proposed that children received 2,000 IU of Vitamin D per day in their first year of life in the 1960s. Then, a great fear of Vitamin D toxicity caused them to drop the amount. First to 1,000 IU, then to just 400 IU. After that unfathomable shift, incidence of type 1 diabetes has doubled over 3 decades.

Nurses were measured for Crohn's disease and ulcerative colitis. The further from the equator these nurses were, the higher their likelihood of both. Arthritis, similarly, falls upon latitude lines. Merlino et al. found that women in Iowa were 30% less likely to develop arthritis when they ate diets high in Vitamin D. Not sunshine, not even supplementation, just dietary choices.

For me, on the autoimmune spectrum for eczema, hay fever, and with very inefficient breathing for most of my life, this is a startling revelation.

Vitamin D Toxicity Fear

In 1950s Britain, an outbreak of hypercalcemia in infants was wrongly attributed to Vitamin D intoxication. This ultimately led to the reduction in Vitamin D fortification and supplementation throughout Europe, as we have seen in Finland's reduction of Vitamin D supplementation in the 1960s. This misplaced paranoia persists today.

Vitamin D toxicity is one of the rarest medical conditions on the planet. It requires extremely consistent, extremely high-dose supplementation. For example, several studies have found that ingesting 1,000,000 IU *daily* for *several months* can raise blood levels of 25(OH)D to more than 500 ng/ml. Ceasing such supplementation often results in a return to normal levels.

To ensure that you don't reach dangerous levels, take a 10,000 IU tablet every 3-6 months.

Breathing & Vitamin D

The most important reason to supplement Vitamin D is to vastly increase the health of your respiratory system. Breathing, before anything else, is the most important action you take every minute of every day. When your airways are inflamed, your body is in a consistently chronic state of stress.

Vitamin D levels play a clear and important role in respiratory health. In the *Breathing* chapter, we looked at how to create a virtuous breathing circle. The virtuous circle of breathing is strengthened significantly by having optimal Vitamin D levels. Vitamin D acts as a powerful shield for the respiratory system.

In the *Hierarchy of Survival*, the biggest factor of life is air. We consume air by breathing. (See *Figure 35*, page 89.) Breathing plays a huge role in how our face develops; both how we breathe and, how much air we consume. We can choose to have optimal Vitamin D levels, to defend and protect our airway and lungs - and for many other health benefits.

Vitamin D has been proven to affect our breathing in several ways, even before we are born. Vitamin D levels of pregnant mothers has been shown to have an impact on the respiratory health of their babies. After birth, the following are all associated with Vitamin D deficiency:

- *Periodontal Disease*
- *Allergic Rhinitis*
- *Chronic Rhinosinusitis*

- *Otitis Media*
- *Acute Respiratory Infections*
- *Adenotonsillar Hypertrophy*
- *Obstructive Sleep Apnoea*
- *Asthma*

With Vitamin D deficiency (less than 20ng/ml) there is a 6-fold increase in respiratory syncytial virus. Upper respiratory tract infections are more common in people with Vitamin D deficiency.

It's common to have seasonal flus and similar contagious respiratory diseases - such as Influenza. When we consider why this might be, we can think about when we get most sunlight. Summer months offer the very best opportunity to naturally increase our levels of Vitamin D. When we move to winter, our Vitamin D levels drop. This is the perfect opportunity for contagious infections to spread. That's why flu season occurs. People who get the flu are low on Vitamin D.[4] Influenza deaths drop dramatically in the summer months. When Vitamin D levels diminish with less sunshine, death rates climb.

Nasal Mucus - How Bad Is a Blocked Nose?

We see blocked noses as a mild inconvenience. The gravity of what is happening is lost on us. I believe that all parents should treat blocked noses with the same seriousness as bleeding. When I child cuts themselves, a good parent will look at the wound, clean it, and if necessary, apply a rudimentary dressing. When a child has a blocked nose, parents tend to ignore it. Whereas most cuts will stop bleeding without intervention, most blocked noses will persist chronically without intervention. Finding which insults trouble the child's immune system and stopping their chronic inflammation is one of the most significant roles for a parent. Unfortunately, most parents believe that a little inflammation is not a big deal.

Do you have a blocked nose? No big deal. Get a tissue. You'll be fine.

A blocked nose is a *nightmare* for your body. This means that you are functioning so poorly that your body must compensate by mouth breathing. Failure to compensate means certain death. Of course, it seems almost silly to make such a statement. How hard can it be to breathe through your mouth to survive? It's easy.

It's easy, but it isn't natural. Your body is forced to use its last resort. This last resort has consequences. It is bad for your health. It is also bad for signs of health. It scars your facial development. People intrinsically see that the environment that you've grown up in was not a healthy one. They see that your ability to thrive in your environment was impaired. The proportions of your face become corrupted. And the more you mouth breathe, the more proportional impairment you suffer.

Nasal blockage occurs for a variety of reasons. How we breathe, breathing efficiency, diet, airborne insults and Vitamin D levels are all large contributing factors. When someone has a blocked nose, all of these factors should be addressed. A blocked nose in childhood is often a defining moment, forming habits – like mouth breathing and atypical swallowing – which impair our potentials for beauty, health and brain performance. A blocked nose can be the catalyst to these potentials being forever lost.

Vitamin D & Me

When I was a boy, we used to go on vacations every few years. Having grown up in the United Kingdom, where the sun is famously mercurial, we'd go to Spain or Italy. Sunlight in these places is stronger and more frequent - especially in the Summer. For each vacation, my mother would be concerned about me getting sunburn.

I once fell asleep on a blow-up lilo airbed in a hotel pool. The Spanish sun shone down brightly. When I awoke, I felt a burn. I pressed my finger into my skin and saw red turn to bone white. I knew that burning was imminent and inescapable.

My brother had a more olive complexion, and he wore less sunscreen. His body was more naturally primed to cope. In my natural climate - overcast Britain - my body adapted to deal with low levels of sunshine for very short periods of time. With school, computer games and stranger-danger, roaming around the neighbourhood was considered unsafe. Indeed, sunshine itself was considered unsafe.

Even when playing with a ball in the garden, I'd hear, "Don't forget to put on sunscreen, or you'll burn." I often did. Because of incidents like this, it was always stressed that I must wear sunscreen.

I was either indoors or wearing sunscreen outside. When I went outside without sun cream, I was exposed to a dose of sunlight that my body was ill-equipped to deal with. So, I'd burn.

For my whole life I was Vitamin D deficient, until I started supplementing Vitamin D and embracing a small amount of daily sunshine. For most people, the requirement for a healthy dose of sunshine is unmet.

When I lived in the tropics, I didn't have hay fever and my skin was clear. My body felt healthier. I put it down to sunshine and salt water, as I swam in the sea a few times a week. I made sure to get 15-30 minutes of sunshine per day without sun cream. If my skin went pink, I'd avoid the sun for a day or two. I felt healthier and I had lower inflammation.

Beauty Is Contagious - The Theory of Propinquity

The Halo Effect[1] - where we assign positive non-physical attributes to the beautiful - is said to be an irrational cognitive bias. It has traditionally been seen as a quirk in our psychology which prompts errors in our judgement. A typical example is employing the physically attractive *Candidate A* over highly experienced *Candidate B*, despite *Candidate B* being better qualified for the role. Yet, that employment decision isn't made just because the employers believe *Candidate A* is better looking. People judge the beautiful to be smarter, more trustworthy and better leaders - even if provided with evidence to the contrary.

What if the *Halo Effect* - and it's even more troubling opposite, the *Horn Effect* - reveal a greater truth about our evolution and development than we previously thought? The *Theory of Propinquity* suggests that our cognitive biases in favour of beauty (Halo) and against ugliness (Horn) are, in fact, hyper-rational. And these biases only make sense if the premise of this book is right - the face is shaped by environmental forces after birth.

Trust is a key element of both political science and the *Halo Effect*. Understanding why we trust one person over another matters. Yet, when we strip away modern hierarchies, like social class and financial success, the overriding attribute that triggers trust becomes quite clear. Remove all variables except for someone's physicality - how they look, move and express themselves - and like clockwork, we're more trusting of the beautiful.

We make decisions about whether to trust someone very quickly. It's been shown repeatedly that we trust more attractive people the most. We feel that beautiful people are worthy of more trust, based purely on how they look. This bias is so powerful and pervasive that trusting attractive people must be an inherited, evolved trait. Trusting more attractive people almost certainly, therefore, helped our species survive.

This trust gives the beautiful a *beauty premium*. But there is a consequence of being attractive and not living up to the extra trust that others place in you. This, like the *Halo Effect* itself, only makes logical sense through the *Theory of Propinquity*. In their study, *Judging a Book by Its Cover: Beauty and Expectations in the Trust Game*,[2] Rick Wilson and

Catherine Eckel found that while there is a *"beauty premium"* with trust, there is also a *"beauty penalty"* when that trust is unfulfilled.

The *Halo* of beauty signals higher intellect, social standing and financial success - but we are far older as a species than the amount of time we had to accrue assets. We have only accrued wealth, job titles and big houses in the last 10,000 or so years (0.4% of human history). The beauty premium - the Halo Effect - predates modern hierarchies. Society, before the shift to asset-accumulation, was egalitarian. As hunters and gatherers - a state humanity has been in for 99.6% of our time on earth[3] - we made important decisions based on instinct.

Before modern times, we used the faces of strangers to decide whether that person was to be trusted or not, without other information. In a world before business cards or expensive clothes, someone's face, body and demeanour were all the information we had. We were remarkably good at quickly assessing who could help us, or who could hinder us. Our lives often depended on it.

The question of why the beauty premium *and* the beauty penalty coexist is quite simple in this hunter gatherer context. When we made decisions to trust people for 99.6% of human existence, it was; to join their social group and follow them; or to allow them to join our group; or for trade. The most important and consequential decision for our ancestors was whether to follow someone or not. That was a leap into the unknown. In evolutionary terms, there is a reason to trust someone who is beautiful. We trust a beautiful face because it can lead us to better *environments* - environments that helped to shape their face.

If the beautiful people we followed were beautiful only because of genetics - if environments didn't affect beauty - there are two possibilities: Our species would have gone extinct hundreds of thousands of years ago; or we wouldn't have evolved to trust the beautiful above others. Being so easily duped into following a beautiful face without the expected payoff of better environments could lead to mortal danger. It would be an evolutionary honey trap.

Allowing the more beautiful to lead us could be a severe hindrance to our survival, not a help, if beauty was pre-set before birth. Following the beautiful to far worse locations would be a gamble. They'd not necessarily live a better way of life than anyone else. In reality, the beautiful *necessarily* live in ways that shape their faces better than the ugly. That's why we trust the beautiful on instinct.

Similarly, if faces were predetermined by genes, our aversion to ugliness would make no sense. We are shaped by our environments. If we were not, we'd have no aversion to the ugly or attraction to the beautiful, because others couldn't impact our development. Only *fertile* humans would care about attraction.

Trusting a beautiful person - especially someone you can't mate with - only makes sense if environmental forces shape faces. We have evolved to sense who grew up in the best environments, with the best habits and lifestyles: The beautiful. And who grew up in the worst environments, with the worst habits and lifestyles: The ugly. Our distrust in the ugly is, tragically, just as pronounced as our trust in the beautiful. The *Horn Effect* is as potent as the *Halo Effect*. The beautiful prompt feelings of compulsion towards them, the ugly prompt feelings of repulsion away from them. While sad, when we accept that faces are malleable, it's hyper-rational.

Sexual Selection Is Overstated

Our evolved trait of following people with better facial development *must be* a consequence of environments and habits shaping faces. Mating opportunities play a part in decisions of where we go and who we follow - but only when we are fertile and see a viable mate. The extent to which sex decisions drive our behaviour is overstated. Why do people favour attractive members of the same sex (who are sexual competition) over the ugly? If mating was the main motivator, and environments didn't shape faces, both sexes would improve their chances of being sexually selected for by surrounding themselves with unattractive friends, so they appear by far the most viable mate. This doesn't commonly occur.

There is evidence that sexual reproduction plays no part in who to trust at all. A study, called *Predicting elections: child's play!*,[4] shows that responses to certain faces are universal. John Antonakis and Olaf Dalgas at the University of Lausanne in Switzerland hoped to determine if election results could be predicted by faces. They collected headshots of candidates from the French 2002 parliamentary elections. 680 adults were asked to pick which candidate looked more competent. All they had to judge was a photo of each candidate's face. Nothing else. The perceived measure of competence predicted the election results 72% of the time.

Now, the interesting part. They changed the question and invited 681 children aged between 5 and 13 years old to participate. Same candidates, same headshots. The question posed was, "*Imagine that you will now sail from Troy to Ithaca. Who would you choose as the captain of your boat?"* The children were 71% accurate at predicting the election results when it was framed as who should lead a mythical voyage.

This, then, is clearly not a choice determined by mating opportunities. If it were, sexual maturity would skew the result. Age causes no measurable difference. This goes against conventional wisdom, but sex is not the primary driving force, and blaming lust would be incredibly naive. Babies stare at beautiful faces for longer.[5] Children and adults assess viable leaders equally. From new-borns to the very oldest in society, we all, innately, favour those who's faces develop well. This, of course, doesn't mean that the winners of the elections are actually more competent. Many elected officials are decidedly incompetent and our judgement for good leaders is often very wrong. Academics believe our assessments of leadership potential in CEOs and politicians are superficial. Yet, Stone Age competence, intelligence and leadership was anything but.

Stone Age Competence Is Written on The Face

Leadership in the Stone Age would include; skill at hunting large, ruminant animals; harvesting honey; foraging skills and avoiding inflammatory foods; finding drinking water; knowing where to go at specific times of year; getting the best levels of exercise and sunshine; and bartering/social skills. Competence was instantly *seen* in someone's facial development.

Skilled hunters would have strong, wide, forward-grown faces from clamp-and-tearing, then chewing tough, fatty meat and roots. They'd chase down large prey over hours or days until the animal collapsed in exhaustion - nose breathing throughout to maintain a clear-headed, relaxed body while maximising athletic ability and oxygen transfer to cells.[6] They'd get ample exercise and sunshine, their muscles would be strong and lean, giving ideal body posture. Their young would be given the same tough food, and they'd be breastfed for far longer due to the toughness of food, making their swallowing action ideal.

A tribe incapable of hunting large, ruminant animals would have relied on foraging. This results in food that was less tough to tear and break down. Less strength and less tearing food with hand and tooth led to less width and less forward growth. Which tribe – the capable or incapable hunters - would you join?

Hunting and living success lent itself to optimal facial development that was seen by all. Living in accordance with nature - developing beautiful faces - was the mark of Stone Age competence and success. We use the same facial cues to assess leadership competence today. The demands on our leaders are completely different, so our assessments are now flawed. That beauty premium - the expectation of preferential outcomes from beautiful people - is irrational in the modern world. Yet in the Stone Age world, for 99.6% of human history, it made absolute sense. Someone beautiful was worth following, learning from, mimicking and looking up to. We'd feel compelled to adopt their habits and lifestyles. This compulsion is still evolved in us, as we mimic celebrities. Mimicking a celebrity fashion craze doesn't help with facial development, of course, but the compulsion to follow - to do what they do and to covet what they have - retains its power. In the world of our ancestors, copying the habits and lifestyles of the beautiful made us and our offspring more beautiful. This is why there exists a beauty premium.

The beauty penalty exists because we have evolved to expect better outcomes from trusting beautiful people. Those better outcomes are implicit in their facial development. Being led somewhere worse for our development and health, by someone beautiful, would leave us feeling duped.

We trust that beautiful people's lifestyles will enhance our health and beauty potentials. When that trust is proved wrong, we feel blindsided. It goes against everything we've evolved to believe. We view the ugly as less trustworthy, less intelligent, less competent, and less worthy of our time because following them would have been dangerous for our development. There is no logic in feeling a strong aversion to something unless it imperils us. Beauty and ugliness must be transmissible through habits and lifestyles, or we wouldn't feel such strong initial reactions, universally.

While our response to physical appearance is frowned upon by many today, in our ancient past it helped us to survive. This leaves only one logical conclusion: Beauty is shaped by environmental factors, or we'd only seek the beautiful (and fear the ugly) when we were in a mating window. Just as a towering warrior might fear a child with smallpox, seeing a child with a very disproportional face would cause similar fears, due to the transmissible nature of facial development.

That the beautiful are good potential mates is an argument for both genetics *and* environment. Genetics and environment must occur together. The beautiful suffer from less inflammation than the less beautiful, generally. Part of this is innate immune system resilience and part is how they live; diet, breathing efficiency, how often they eat, amount of exercise and sunshine, mouth posture, etc. Although some have more resilient immune systems, autoimmunity is provoked by lifestyle factors.

The *Halo Effect argument* goes that beautiful people are not worthy of more trust, or of leadership roles, or of being perceived as more intelligent. Looks don't account for how trustworthy, or competent, or smart someone is. The *halo* makes them appear better in areas unrelated to looks. Yet, there was wisdom in trusting the beautiful and assigning them as leaders. We subconsciously use beauty as a sign that those who possess it come from good environments and habits - they most closely followed the Beauty Quadrant. Those environments lead to healthier people, with less cognitive or physical impairment. Following the beautiful, therefore, was a viable and compelling survival strategy.

Why Do We Assume the Beautiful Are More Intelligent?

We can begin to understand why we trust the beautiful, give them leadership roles and follow them. What of intelligence? Surely, there is no real basis for this aspect of the *Halo Effect* in today's world. Research suggests that more attractive people *are* more intelligent.[7] The common reasoning for this is because women are attracted to intelligence and men are attracted to beauty. The offspring of a smart man and a beautiful woman are more likely to benefit from both attributes. This is logical.

However, it's not quite that simple. We are all born with high health and beauty potentials. The less beautiful have deviated *away* from their potentials. When we deviate away from proper facial development, we are also more likely to suffer from sleep apnoea and other health issues. Sleep apnoea is a symptom of craniofacial maldevelopment; where the bones and muscles in your face and head have developed wrongly, shrinking your airway and disrupting breathing in your sleep. The impact of sleep apnoea on the IQ and cognitive ability of children has been measured:

> *Children with OSA [Obstructive Sleep Apnoea] had lower mean IQ test scores (85) than children without OSA (101). Children with OSA also performed worse on standardized tests measuring executive functions, such as verbal working memory (8 versus 15) and word fluency (9.7 versus 12).[8]*

Improper facial development impacts the brain in negative ways, through intelligence, mood, and neurological disorders. Its consequences go far beyond beauty. Not only are those who suffer from sleep apnoea less attractive, less happy and less healthy, they are also less smart. The wording here is important. It's not that the beautiful gain intelligence. It's that the improperly shaped - those with less efficient bodies and less well-developed faces - lose intelligence due to developed inefficiencies. Any mother will tell you that a child who isn't well-rested becomes more difficult. They find it harder to concentrate, to listen, to behave, and to learn. This is the reality - every day, for life - when a body becomes less efficient through permanent facial changes caused by improper environments.

Are Attractive People Healthier?

For the *Theory of Propinquity* to be correct, the beautiful must be healthier too, as beauty and health potentials are entwined. And so, it proves. A University of Cincinnati study[9] looked at 15,000 people, rated their attractiveness and their medical records. They also conducted a 90-minute interview for each person. Participants were graded on their physical attractiveness on a scale of 1 to 5.

The study found that for each step up on the attractiveness scale, men were 13% less likely to suffer from high cholesterol. Someone who was rated as a level 5 in attraction was 13% less likely to have high cholesterol that a level 4, etc. For high blood pressure, each step represented a 20% difference in probability. Each step represented a 15% reduction in depression, a 23% reduction in ADHD and a 21% reduction of stuttering.

In women, each step up in attractiveness represented a 21% reduction in high blood pressure; a 22% reduction in diabetes; a 12% reduction in asthma; a 17% reduction in clinical depression; an 18% reduction in ADHD; an 18% reduction in stuttering; and a 13% reduction in tinnitus.

Women who were rated as very attractive were approximately half as likely to suffer from most of these issues as very unattractive women. For both sexes, beautiful people are less likely to have sick days, chronic disease or neuropsychological disorders. The only instances of attractive people being more likely to suffer from medical conditions is through sexually transmitted infections.

Optimal development leads to beauty and better health outcomes. People who have no/low inflammation are more likely to develop beautifully, as they're more likely to adhere to the Beauty Quadrant. The *Cincinnati Study* shows us that we can read human faces, and the Theory of Propinquity suggests that our beauty bias exists because environments, habits and lifestyles shape our faces, our beauty and our health. It's no surprise to learn that science suggests attractive people[10] and intelligent people[11] live longer.

Our hunter gatherer ancestors lived in a world where the Beauty & Health Quadrants were naturally adhered to every day; their environments catered for them. Today, our lives have strayed astronomically far from our natural environments. Yet, environmental forces still shape modern faces.

Our innate, universal, cradle-to-grave biases only make sense if facial development is contagious through habits and lifestyles.

Hollywood Reflects the Theory of Propinquity

Hollywood movies mirror our biases with their casting decisions. The difference between heroes and heroines versus villains in cinema is usually one of airway space and jaw strength.

Take Disney's *Cinderella*. Cinderella, the heroine, has a well-proportioned face. Her jaws are grown forward. Her airway large. Her stepmother, the villain, has jaws that are set back and a long, protruding chin and a nose made more prominent by a recessed maxilla. Her face has grown down. Her airway is far smaller because of this compromise in facial growth.

Cinderella's evil stepmother is seen indoors in the shade (low vitamin D), often sitting in bed (low exercise), and has a cat (allusion to allergy and airway inflammation). These details aren't just a trope of someone who is inherently unkind. They are environmental factors that cause a face to become developmentally impaired. The one thing that the evil stepmother is missing in the animation - considering her face shape - is consistent mouth breathing.

Through the lens of the *Hierarchy of Survival* - a large airway is healthier - and the Theory of Propinquity, it's clear to see why we root for the optimal facial proportions of Cinderella and against her evil stepmother. Even young children understand who to root for on sight alone. We want to be around people who show, physically, that their environment was optimal for facial development. We like those who develop optimally, and we mistrust those who don't. This is as true in the courtroom as in the cinema. Attractive people who are proved guilty of a crime are given lighter punishments than less attractive people.[12]

Hollywood exploits our biases. Advertisers do too. Products are seen as part of the environments, habits and lifestyles of the beautiful models and celebrities who promote them. Our brains are still wired as Stone Age man, believing innately that mimicry of the beautiful may reflect on our own faces, despite all logic to the contrary. Such is the power of environments over facial development.

The Corruption Of The Health Quadrant

The biggest enemy of the Health Quadrant, chronic inflammation, can corrupt our ability to hold natural mouth posture. It is heavily affected by what we eat. Many foods can inflame us. The most inflamed and ill among us wilt and weaken physically (and mentally) with each passing day.

Several prominent researchers have put our facial degradation down to what we eat. Charles Darwin recognised that soft, cooked food caused jaws to shorten. This concerns both what we eat and how we eat. Weston Price believed that what we ate alone, and the lack of nutrients in mass-produced food, caused facial degeneration. He was a dentist who practiced between World Wars I & II in the United States. He visited five continents in the 1930s after becoming worried about the number of crooked and decaying teeth at his Ohio practice. His research was profoundly detailed, although his conclusion was flawed.

Price had a natural control group in each society he visited. He studied "isolated" communities and "modernized" communities. The isolated communities lived a pre-industrial lifestyle. These were the controls. The modernised communities lived a post-industrial lifestyle. Price compared isolated and modernized groups in Swiss, Gaelic, Inuit, North American Indian, Melanesian, Polynesian, African, Australian Aboriginal, Torres Strait Islander, New Zealand Māori and Peruvian Indian communities. He photographed the differences in each community.

Isolated communities - irrespective of race, climate and geographical location - all had wide dental arches, straight teeth, no tooth decay and wide, short faces. In modernized communities, he found narrow dental arches, crooked teeth, severe tooth decay and longer, narrower faces. The evidence was clear, a shift to modern lifestyles caused radical changes in teeth and faces.

In his book, *Nutrition and Physical Degeneration*, Price suggests that this shift was due to the lack of nutrition in modern, post-industrial diets. To Price, nutrition (and nutrition alone) caused malocclusion and facial degeneration. In all the "modernized" communities, everywhere he visited, Price saw, *"very definite and typical changes represented by the narrowing of the features and the lengthening of the face with crowding of the teeth in the arch."*[1]

Some of his peers argued that these changes were hereditary traits. In response to a colleague suggesting malocclusion was passed through generations, Price confidently asserts:

"all of the distortions of the face and jaws which he presents as being related to heredity can be duplicated, as I have shown, in the disturbances appearing in the first and second generation after... [indigenous societies] have adopted the foods of our modern civilizations in displacement of their native foods."[2]

Price didn't see the shift from uncooked to cooked meals. He was born in 1870, a year before Darwin's *Descent of Man* was published. In Price's life, most meals were cooked and eaten with knives and forks. The change Price saw was a shift to processed foods, grains and sugars.

He noted that readers of his work, *Nutrition And Physical Degeneration*, will see in a *"large... percentage of white [post-industrial] families the progressive narrowing and lengthening of the face in the younger members of the family as compared with the older."*[3] The book was published in 1938. A stark dietary shift occurred from his generation to his children's generation.

Just as, in 1871, Darwin and three of his peers from different continents saw jaws shorten (become recessed), and ~100 years before that the overbite began as cutlery-use became ubiquitous, another rapid and endemic change in facial development was afoot. As societies moved further away from fulfilling their facial environmental expectations, and further into the clutches of modern life, Price saw the narrowing and lengthening of faces in real time. This was partly due to the damage to the Health Quadrant that processed foods and modern living caused.

Price's photographs highlight that no isolated group had need for braces. Every modernised group needed them. This was consistent across every country. This shift to longer, narrower faces occurred to children born from the early 20th Century.

While Price believed that nutrients keep faces proportional, the reality is more complex. Anti-nutrients in certain plants can cause inflammation. This triggers an autoimmune cascade in some, but not all, of us which results in blocked noses (causing mouth breathing), inflammation in the airways (causing breathing inefficiency and asthma), and inflammation throughout the body as inflammatory food punctures through the gut wall, into the bloodstream and beyond. This cascade is an indirect threat to our beauty potential, as maintaining correct form becomes difficult or impossible.

What we eat plays a role in inflammation, which is why it is the second Health Quadrant, but diet isn't the only reason for inflammation. How we breathe and how much we breathe can inflame us; it is the first Health Quadrant. Our level of fitness, and our Vitamin D levels act as a shield against inflammation and make up the final two Health Quadrants.

While the Health Quadrant can seriously inhibit our ability to maintain the Beauty Quadrant, those with no inflammation who don't maintain mouth posture, swallow correctly, eat tough foods or maintain proper body posture still lose beauty potential.

A Lucky Few People Never Get Inflamed

Some people have zero negative inflammatory side effects from what they eat. They have no inflammation markers in their blood and no physical manifestations of inflammation. For those people, diets can be viewed in a more traditional sense. Their aims should be to maintain a healthy weight and sustain their bodies with a variety of healthy foods.

Whereas a sufferer of Celiac disease shouldn't eat a slice of bread, even once a month, some can eat bread daily with no negative consequences whatsoever. The task then becomes to figure out if you are prone to inflammation, and the insults (foods) which affect you personally.

Are Declines in Health Due to Ageing?

Declines in health are often put down to age. Age in itself isn't the driving factor in many illnesses. As with breathing and mouth posture affecting the airway and the face, the important factors are pressure and time. The accumulation of constant autoimmune attacks is where pressure and time converge to cause damage.

There are two brackets in time where our potentials and vulnerabilities are shaped. The first is our beauty potential, which lasts from birth to about 15 years old. This is the most important time to maximise your potential for beauty and to ensure you have a large airway. The much longer bracket is your level of inflammation. This is a lifelong bracket. It occurs from birth to death. Inflammation can begin at any time. The damage, if left unchecked, will accumulate until you develop chronic conditions caused by constant attacks on healthy cells. The shift in diets - from natural to more modern - can, and often does, lead to facial maldevelopment and health consequences which blight us throughout our lives.

When your body is focused on quelling daily attacks, it has less energy to focus on keeping other cells healthy. More stress on your body, if everything else is equal, means faster ageing. Your immune system is weakened by constant action, not constant inaction. When it is constantly active, it neglects "spring cleaning" to focus on bigger and more imminent threats.

"Beauty is Genetic!" Is False

The genetics-only beauty argument is pervasive today, but it's inaccurate. Families often look very similar, because of both genetics and environmental forces. *Epigenetics* causes genes to switch on or off in changing environments, such as skin getting darker after sunbathing.

There is a facial growth blueprint, which changes *epigenetically* under different environmental stressors. As a result, we either retain ideal facial proportions or we lose them. Family-wide facial disproportion is caused by environmental vulnerabilities in the Beauty and Health Quadrants. When families retain proportion and beauty, their genes have expressed their *potentials* - as the environmental expectations of facial development have been met - rather than exposing their *vulnerabilities*. Parents and children live very similar lifestyles, so often, but not always, they have similar levels of beauty and health.

Let's take asthma as an example of a vulnerability. Asthma is one of many autoimmune conditions where the body exists in a state of chronic inflammation. Asthma is a disaster for the Health Quadrant, as the body is chronically inflamed. It's perhaps the biggest disaster for the Beauty Quadrant too, as most asthma sufferers are unable to maintain natural mouth posture because they mouth-breathe. If one parent is asthmatic, their child has a 25% of being asthmatic. If both parents are, that rises to 50%.[4]

Many attribute asthma solely to genetics. The percentages above show this to be untrue. Predisposition is not predetermination. Genetic vulnerability is one of three necessities for autoimmune conditions such as asthma to form. The other two - an inflammation trigger and intestinal permeability - are environmental. Asthma and other autoimmune issues can't take hold unless all three conditions are met. Remove inflammation triggers and intestinal permeability and you remove the opportunity for vulnerabilities to be expressed.

Families pass down both genetics and lifestyles - particularly the foods that both insult the immune system and cause intestinal permeability. These environmental factors are simple to remove. There is one factor that isn't caused by a weakened Health Quadrant - habits. Some families pass down habits that impact the Beauty Quadrant without being on the autoimmune spectrum. A child, who looks up adoringly to their mouth-breathing parent, may mimic them and form the habit themselves. Negative habits are a direct attack on the Beauty Quadrant, without the Health Quadrant being an accomplice.

Some people are born with stronger immune systems to protect against facial disproportion. However, communities only started seeing jaw problems when their diets and lifestyles became Westernized. There is no evidence of humans suffering from bad bites and crooked teeth before the agricultural revolution ~10,000 years ago. It became far more common after the industrial revolution, which began 250 years ago. Changes to facial development have been recorded across whole societies in one generation when those societies adopted Westernised lifestyles. These environmental changes exposed vulnerabilities to our Beauty & Health Quadrants, not predetermined genetics.

The "beauty is genetic" argument feels obvious in many instances, but completely perplexing in others. When we see very beautiful parents having very beautiful children, we think they have a wonderful, deep gene pool. When we see unattractive children borne of unattractive parents, it confirms the genetic argument more.

The thesis loses weight when very beautiful people have unattractive offspring and unattractive people have very beautiful offspring. Many families have siblings where one is beautiful, and another is not. How can we account for those differences when the genetics and environments passed down are so similar? Being lucky is not a reasonable answer.

The accurate answer is simple: The beautiful offspring, in every case, consistently applied the Beauty Quadrant and the unattractive offspring did not. Someone's beauty directly relates to how consistently they apply the Beauty Quadrant. It could be as simple as one child breathing through their mouth and another nose-breathing. It could be to do with allergies, or even the toughness of food each child favours. This is how startling differences in beauty from the very same parents occurs. Maintain the Beauty Quadrant and you retain facial beauty. When the immune system of one child in a family is triggered, but the other child's is not, this causes a *Health Quadrant* disruption, which then affects the *Beauty Quadrant*. In these cases, those with allergies and intolerances are often not only less healthy, but also less beautiful.

Does this go against Darwinism? Not at all. Facial disproportion occurs when there are big shifts in how we live. Since the agricultural revolution, then the industrial revolution, there have been many changes that affected facial form. Charles Darwin himself noticed facial changes from one of these developments; jaws growing less forwards from eating soft, cooked foods. Darwin and his contemporaries shared their findings in their correspondences, and Darwin highlights this exact phenomenon in his book, *The Descent of Man*. Darwin correctly attributed the facial changes he witnessed to jaws not chewing enough tough foods. He recognised that changing habits, not predetermined genetics, was the cause of the descent of jaw form.

Do Genetics Play Any Role?

> *'All happy families are alike; each unhappy family is unhappy in its own way.' Anna Karenina, Leo Tolstoy*

Tolstoy's quotation about familial happiness could just as easily be applied to facial development. Happy families are happy because of the emotional environmental forces of love, respect and compassion. Well-formed faces are well-formed when they adhere to the physical environmental forces already discussed. All well-formed faces have very similar proportions, yet poorly formed faces have widely differing proportions. Faces that grow properly adhere to the natural proportions that signify health and good looks. Our genes offer a roadmap of growth. Families have similar *features* - skin colour, hair, eye colour - because of their similar genetics. But individual family members are more or less attractive because of how physical environmental forces shape their faces in proportion, symmetry and sexual dimorphism (how masculine men's faces are and how feminine women's faces are.)

Snowflakes offer a similar example. Every snowflake is different, but they all obey the same natural laws as they form - a strict pattern of six-fold symmetry.[5] There is an underlying law which shapes them all on their journey to the ground. The six arms are all the same length, and you can draw a perfect circle around them. They obey the same fundamental hexagonal proportions, even though their features can be very different. We don't find warped snowflakes - such as oblong, or 7 sided snowflakes - because the environmental requirements to form perfect, proportional snowflakes always exist.

Unlike snowflakes, humanity is seeing a corruption of natural laws when we form. Whereas all snowflakes retain their proportion, our faces do not. Just like a snowflake, the pressures on us shape us until we reach maturity. But humans in the last 250 years have lost our facial proportions. Most faces these days don't retain perfect proportions. Instead, our faces are like warped snowflakes.

Genetics can protect your *Health Quadrant* from corruption in the modern world. As we have seen with the asthma example, while genetics play no direct role in applying the Beauty Quadrant, they can impact the Health Quadrant when genetically vulnerable people are exposed to triggers. This, in turn, affects the *Beauty Quadrant*. Stronger immune systems - which don't react to food-borne or air-borne insults - support the Beauty Quadrant, but weaker immune system can corrupt it. In this sense, luck is involved. For those who are unlucky, removing things that insult the immune system is key to maintaining the Health Quadrant.

When societies shift from ancestral lifestyles to modern ones, issues of facial proportion and overall health sprout without fail. This is not genetic devolution. It's always provoked by dramatic changes to the Beauty and Health Quadrants. Those who still emerge beautiful in modern societies, do so because they are able to apply the Beauty Quadrant. Often, they aren't afflicted with the chronic inflammation that indirectly causes beauty loss.

The genetics-only argument becomes harmful when we aren't teaching people that environmental factors have a huge impact on facial development, which in turn directly impacts long-term health. When the face doesn't grow proportionally, the nasal cavity and sinuses have too little space to effectively protect the respiratory and immune systems. This becomes a compounding problem which loses beauty and health potentials over time. Jaws growing wrongly leads to life-shortening complications like sleep apnoea, which can take a decade off people's lives. This doesn't occur when facial environmental expectations are met and faces experience proportional, forwards growth.

A beautiful face - a face that has developed proportionally in adulthood - leads to a healthier life than a less proportional face. Aiming for proper facial development is important for health, longevity and the societal benefits of being more attractive.

Healthy People Have Beautiful Faces & Disproportion Leads to Ill Health

The University of Cincinnati study (see *Beauty is Contagious – The Theory of Propinquity*) shows that the most beautiful are far healthier than the least beautiful. Beauty leads to better health outcomes. People who have no inflammation are more likely to develop beautifully as the Health Quadrant supports the Beauty Quadrant. The Beauty Quadrant is much harder to maintain - mouth posture, swallowing, how you eat and body posture - when you are inflamed due to unhealthy breathing, dietary, exercise and vitamin D habits. This is how health is seen through beauty. The most beautiful maintain the Beauty Quadrant and the least beautiful find it impossible to do so. The *Cincinnati Study* shows us that we can read human faces and beauty signifies better health. Those who thrive in their childhood environments become more beautiful and healthy.

A new-born baby always sleeps with their mouth closed. Equally, babies are not born with high blood pressure, asthma or diabetes - these symptoms occur when the immune system becomes compromised. They develop due to triggers that we consume from what we eat and the air we breathe. These conditions, therefore, are as preventable as ugliness itself. But, untreated, they put the body under stress.

Someone could have a genetic predisposition to a food insult, which cascades into eczema, asthma and hay fever - as the body is on high alert for insults in food and the air. But predisposition is not predetermination. Just as we can avoid needing snake anti-venom by avoiding snake bites, we can avoid the inflammatory cascade by avoiding inflammatory foods, and by becoming exclusively low-volume nose breathers.

Continual stress to our respiratory and digestive systems (through overbreathing and poor diet) leads to worse health and beauty outcomes. When one area is chronically inflamed, everywhere else in the body is more prone to inflammation and autoimmune damage. The immune system is poor at differentiating between parts of the body. For example, when some people eat wheat, they get a blocked nose. Clearly a food trigger shouldn't activate a shield (mucus) for airborne triggers; yet it does. The body doesn't know any better.

Chronic inflammation or habits of bad posture cause the face to lose its proportions which dramatically affects health. Beauty potential damages health potential, or, to put it another way, long-term poor form causes long-term poor function through smaller airways. This works both ways. Poor function (through a weak Health Quadrant) can cause poor form, as inflamed airways can lead to mouth breathing and beauty loss.

The health implications of facial disproportion are far-reaching and profound. Most people in modern societies have recessed jaws. A sure sign that someone has developmental issues is the need for braces. Crooked teeth and recessed or misaligned jaws only occur when the environmental expectations for teeth, jaws and faces are unmet. This is typically caused in all four sections of the Beauty Quadrant. It is a sign of bigger problems. Skeletally, you will be compromised. Facial bones remodel and compensate, leaving a less attractive, less efficient face. Crooked teeth and misaligned, recessed jaws are common, but they are not normal.

Those with disproportional faces are more likely to have ENT (ear, nose and throat) issues. These include glue ear, tonsilitis, sinusitis and a deviated nasal septum. Incidentally, this is why tinnitus most frequently occurs in the least attractive. Ear, nose and throat spaces are pinched. They lose natural proportion, and function worse because of it.

They are more likely to suffer from Temporomandibular disorder (TMD): Problems with the joints and muscles needed to chew. When your jaw bones remodel due to a weak foundation, you can be afflicted by jaw pain and discomfort. You might also develop problems with your neck and upper back. Your face will be longer, thinner and less attractive.

Snoring is a common symptom of too-small airways combined with overbreathing. Recessed jaws cause pinched airways, which leads to snoring and *obstructive sleep apnoea (OSA)*. Dr. David Gozal, MD. says, "Snoring is not normal and snoring should never occur!" Our pre-farming ancestors had large airways and well-developed faces. Snoring and sleep apnoea are - like diabetes, heart disease and facial disproportion - modern epidemics.

Perhaps the biggest issue of all is sleep apnoea. John Remmers MD suggests that sleep apnoea is becoming the most common chronic disease in all industrialized countries.[1] It's also the most dangerous inflammatory health issue that many people contend with. Here are the dangers of sleep apnoea:

- Depression
- Memory Loss
- Acid Reflux
- Brain Fog

- Adult Asthma
- Weak Immune System
- High Blood Pressure
- Breathing Issues
- Heart Problems
- Liver Problems
- Lower Libido
- Lower Fertility
- Low Blood Oxygen Levels
- High Cholesterol
- Fatigue
- High Blood Sugar
- Type 2 Diabetes
- Heart Disease
- Fatty liver disease
- Liver Scarring
- Overabundance of liver enzymes
- Gastroesophageal reflux Disease (GERD)
- Obesity & Weight Gain
- Abnormal Heart Rhythm
- Stroke
- Heart Failure
- Dry Mouth & Sore Throat
- Halostis
- Headaches
- Lack of Focus
- Irritability

This list is terrifying in both scope and prevalence. It's no surprise that sleep apnea can take up to 18 years off your life. All of these issues are more likely when a face doesn't develop properly. Sleep apnea occurs when the muscles in the airway relax and the airway closes, halting breathing until the body reacts. In severe cases, breathing is halted more than 30 times an hour. This puts the body under constant stress; inflammation reigns freely. Lifespans are cut short when sleep apnea prevails. When people develop wider airways, sleep apnea is far less likely to occur.

The number of stroke patients who suffer from OSA is between 65%-80%. It's a condition that affects 17% of Americans, at least. John Remmers also suggests that 95% of OSA patients haven't been diagnosed!

Who are the people least likely to snore? You'd expect it to be young people. Unfortunately, it's not children. Dr Gozal estimates that 7%-13% of preschool children snore and 2%-3% of children are suffering from OSA. The most beautiful people, whose faces are wide, with forward projection, are the least likely to snore. They have large airways and plenty of room in their mouths. They have always had impeccable resting mouth posture - even in sleep. They are more efficient with the amount of air they require each minute of every day.

Dr Bill Hang, a Californian orthodontist, has spent his life creating larger airways in his orthodontic patients. He believes that dentistry should focus on prevention of heart disease, Parkinson's, strokes, cancer, dementia, diabetes, head & face pain and many other diseases.[2] He is an exception in his field. All orthodontists should focus on forward and lateral growth of the maxilla and increasing airway size. Yet, they tend to do the opposite - shrinking mouths and airways by using retractive braces that pull the jaws backwards. This further feeds the epidemic of snoring and sleep apnea.

We all dislike the sound of snoring. There is good reason for that. It's unnatural. When we were hunter gathers, snoring was an immediate threat, attracting predators. In modern times, it affects the quality of our sleep, and the quality of our partner's sleep. Even, perhaps, the quality of our whole family's sleep. Snoring is *common*, yet it's not *natural*. It's a common occurrence that should never naturally occur. It wouldn't occur if our faces were properly developed. When a face is forward grown and someone is very efficient with air, snoring doesn't take place.

What becomes clear the more you think about how adaptable we are is that looks aren't the only thing that gets worse. We sound worse; such as when we snore or breathe loudly. We feel worse; skin conditions - from acne to eczema - are the result of chronic inflammation. We smell worse; the bacteria *Helicobacter pylori* exists in inflamed guts and causes bad breath.[3] Our strong reactions to others, provoked through our senses of sight, sound, touch and smell suggests something quite profound; beauty and health potentials and deficiencies are *transmissible* through learning.

Defining Facial Beauty

Facial beauty involves three main attributes; proportion, symmetry and sexual dimorphism.

Proportion is the ratios of facial features to each other. These proportions are directly retained or lost through the Beauty Quadrant. We can measure how proportional a face is using the Marquardt Beauty Mask.

Symmetry is how similar the right half of the face is to the left half. The more symmetrical a face is, the more attractive it is. Like proportion, this is also dictated by the Beauty Quadrant.

Sexual Dimorphism is how masculine or feminine a face is. For men, the ideal is a more masculine face. For women, the ideal is a more feminine face. This is dictated by sex hormone release during puberty, which is driven by the Health Quadrant.

Proportion: The Marquardt Beauty Mask

The Marquardt Beauty Mask (MBM) is a mask which, when overlaid on a person's face, fits beautiful faces exceptionally well. It's based on the proportions of beauty and was created by Dr Steven Marquardt, to show the facial ratios of the beautiful. The mask applies to all people of all races. The geometry of beautiful faces is cross-cultural. It's also cross-generational. It fits anyone beautiful, of any era and any race. People who adhere closest to the MBM are considered more beautiful than people whose faces deviate from it. There is a male version and a female version as male and female proportions are slightly different - due to sexual dimorphism.

Ideal proportions occur when someone conforms to the environmental forces found in the *Beauty Quadrant*. Less conformity causes bone remodelling. This leads to a less proportional, less beautiful face.

Proportions are where facial beauty exists, not features. Beautiful features are highlighted by proper proportions. Beauty potential is lost when proportions are lost, through bone remodelling due to negative pressure over time.

We know that an Irish native looks dramatically different to an Ethiopian native. Yet, take an image of the most beautiful people from any culture, at any time in history, and the mask fits almost perfectly. This even holds true in statues from ancient Egypt, Greece and Rome.

We all intrinsically see the geometries that are most beautiful. We are born with the ability to instantly spot beauty. People believe beauty is a gift from God; that it's predetermined and a fleeting few of us are blessed with it. This is false.

Beauty is caused.

Where all beautiful faces conform to the Marquardt Beauty Mask, all unattractive faces don't. When we apply the Marquardt Beauty Mask to pictures of hunter-gatherer tribal faces, it fits them far better than many modern people. They got the positive environmental pressures that we have evolved to expect. These pressures shaped their faces beautifully, retaining their beauty potential.

On our website you can find the Marquardt Beauty Mask with links to images and apps that allow you to check how closely you conform to the proportions of beauty. We also show examples of how the most famous faces in the world today and statues from history all conform to these proper proportions.

On the face, proportions interact with proportions. It has long been known that there is a repeating ratio in nature. The Golden Ratio is 1 to 1.618. These are the general proportions. For example, the top of the head to the chin versus the width of the head should be 1.618. If the width of the base of the nose is 1, the width of the mouth should be 1.618. The distance from outer eye to outer eye is 1.618, where the width of the mouth is 1. These proportions are retained by applying nature's expected forces to the face, just like the perfect 6-fold symmetry of ever snowflake.

The Golden Ratio - Phi

Nature adheres to this specific ratio in startling ways. The Golden Ratio follows the Fibonacci sequence. The sequence - which begins 0, 1, 1, 2, 3, 5, 8, 13, 21, 34, 55 - follows that each number is the sum of the two numbers which precede it. The ratio as you go deeper in the sequence is also called Phi, or 1:1.618. Even DNA, the building block of life, measures 34 angstroms long by 21 angstroms wide per cycle of the double helix spiral. From something as small as DNA, we also see the ratios in things as massive as spiral galaxies. Spiral shells conform to it, as do pinecones, sunflower seeds, flower petals, tree branches, honey bee bodies, even animal flight patterns.

In humans, the length of your forearm is 1.618, where the length of your hand from the wrist to fingertips is 1. The length from the floor to your navel when standing is 1.618 where the length from your navel to the top of your head is 1. When order triumphs over chaos, the integrity of the golden ratio is retained.

In facial terms, chaos is when form and function are compromised. Order is where environmental expectations are met, and the Golden Ratio is retained.

Facial Width and Height

The overall proportion of a face - as measured by width (1) to height (1.618) - is perhaps the most significant ratio of all. People who retain a properly proportioned facial width-to-height ratio tend to retain beautiful proportions in their other features. A fitting analogy is if a delivery box is undamaged, its contents is more likely to be undamaged too. Retaining the ideal facial width to height proportion makes all other proportions more easily maintained.

For example, the proportion under the eye to the middle of the lips is 1.618, where the distance from the middle of the lips to the chin is 1. From the upper most vertical line of the mask to the bottom of the nose represents 1.618, where the distance from the bottom of the nose to the chin is 1. When we encourage forward growth (thereby inhibiting vertical growth) these proportions are not lost.

Facial width is far less variable than facial height. Yet, the cheekbones will be wider set when the maxilla grows forwards and to the sides. Our jaw muscles and our tongue, when mouth posture is properly applied, cause the upper jaw to grow forwards, and the upper dental arch to be wide. Those mouth posture forces meet the environmental expectation of our face. Failure to maintain mouth posture allows our beauty potential to slip away, and the 1:1.618 ratio of width to facial height shifts to a less healthy and aesthetic ratio.

Lower Jaw Width

Consider an invisible, unmovable support under the chin. In a growing jaw, with such a support in place, growth can only occur forwards from your face, and out to the sides. The support completely eradicates the potential for vertical, downwards growth. The jaw must grow, support or no support. Growing forwards and out to the sides is what occurs when mouth posture is correctly applied. Your tongue and your lower jaw act as the invisible support.

Now imagine that under-chin support is completely taken away. All of a sudden, the jaw can grow downwards. Vertical growth means that forwards growth and sideways growth are inhibited. This affects both jaw width and jaw height in negative ways. Those Golden Ratio proportions are lost. Vertical, downward growth also shrinks the size of the airway. This doesn't just affect the lower jaw, it also affects the maxilla which spans from under the eyes to the upper jaw. It affects the cheekbones, which are lifted up by a high, forward-grown maxilla and which droop down when the maxilla drops.

Lateral Proportions

The width of the nose is a ratio of 1 when the width of the mouth is 1.618. Indeed, the flat part of the chin is also a ratio of 1, as is the width of each eye, and the distance between eyebrows. The width of each eyebrow is 1.618. The distance from the side of the mouth to the edge of the face horizontally (where your lower jaw muscles are) is 1. The distance from the side of the nose to the edge of the face is 1.618. These dimensions appear across the face. They can only occur when the forces that the body expects are applied as we grow.

Averageness

Proportions and features which attract us most are surprising in their *averageness*. Nothing is too big, nothing is too small. Everything is proportionally average to everything else at the ratio of 1:1.618. The remarkable aspect of beauty is that we find averageness exceptional and exceptions to averageness plain or ugly.

In evolutionary biology, the word *koinophilia* is used to describe this phenomenon. Philia - meaning fondness - and koinos - meaning common, or average. This fondness of the average leads to mates choosing common features over odd ones.

When you take lots of faces from each culture and morph them together, they err towards averageness, and they tend to be more beautiful than virtually all of the pictures involved in the morph. The first person to do this was Francis Galton - cousin of Charles Darwin - in 1883. He wanted to see if faces of criminals and vegetarians each had typical characteristics. He discovered that the composite images were more attractive, as they morph towards the Golden Ratio.

fWHR

Facial Width to Height Ratio (fWHR) is a fairly accurate measure of facial beauty. Generally, the higher the ratio of width of the cheekbones across the face, compared to the height of the face from the eyebrow to the upper lip, the better. Studies have found that women favour short-term lovers with a high fWHR. It has been associated with higher testosterone levels.

fWHR reveals certain things. Firstly, the nasal cavity and maxillary sinuses are wide. Second, downwards growth hasn't occurred. Thirdly, the cheekbones are projected wide - this highlights maxillary forwards growth, and is a sign of attractiveness in and of itself.

Symmetry

Symmetry is the second factor in measuring a beautiful face. Those who retain symmetry are seen as more attractive than those who don't. Symmetry is defined by how closely one side of the face looks like the other.

Asymmetry risk increases through inbreeding, premature birth, psychosis and mental retardation.[1] All of these can be explained by form and function. Inbreeding makes people's immune systems weak. Premature birth means that babies are born in extreme stress. Psychosis and mental retardation tend to mean that the forces applied at rest are inconsistent.

For people who are born without such issues, we still see asymmetry, as discussed previously in the *Asymmetry Shows That Facial Forces Matter* section (page 86). Asymmetry becomes worse as we age, through *"asymmetric skeletal remodelling... and the descent of the soft tissue."*[2] However, it's not evenly distributed throughout the population, as people with a strong Beauty Quadrant better maintain their proportions and symmetry.

Observers inherently understand that a stroke - where muscles on one half of a face go limp - can cause facial asymmetry. Indeed, the jaws and teeth of stroke victims often become misaligned. Yet, those same observers often believe that faces are predetermined to look as they do. Those two beliefs can't logically coexist. Either muscles - their use, their strength and their posture - can affect a face, or it can't. Those who believe that faces and beauty are predetermined would have to take incredible leaps of logic to explain the fact that strokes change faces.

The only explanation for a stroke changing a face is muscle loss on one side of the face. If one tragic event changes a face in negative ways, then accrued pressure over a lifetime clearly does too.

Asymmetry is a result of inconsistent forces on the face. It can occur for a number of reasons. Mouth posture is the primary reason. How you eat and chew, and what you eat - soft food or tough food - is second. How you swallow is third.

If someone applies more pressure with the tongue to the left side of their palate than the right, or tilts their head to one side and mouth breathes, this will lead to asymmetry, loss of proportions and possibly lower levels of sex hormones being released at puberty. Chewing on one side of the mouth only will lead to different muscle strength on either side of the lower jaw. This causes differences across the face. The body compensates under unexpected pressures to remodel the face. These facial compensations occur through epigenetic regulation - the body creates a revised roadmap to change bone and tissue growth. Sadly, inconsistent forces lead to asymmetrical faces, loss of attractiveness and all the issues associated with lost beauty.

Sexual Dimorphism

Men have a different beauty mask to women due to sexual dimorphism. When we reach puberty, the differences between boys and girls becomes far more pronounced. The release of sex hormones changes facial proportions, voices, bodies and thoughts.

It's often been thought that sexual dimorphism is as predetermined as facial proportion. Our levels of inflammation at pubescent age defines how much sex hormone we get during puberty. More inflammation means less sex hormone, which means less sexual dimorphism.

How Sex Hormones Affect the Face

Men see growth of their lower jaw, cheekbones, brow ridges, the area from the brow to the bottom of the nose, and facial hair. Generally, men's lips become thinner. Men's facial bones grow more when sex hormones are released during puberty.

For women, facial growth is limited. This is typically why very feminine women's features are smaller and more delicate. The nose and jaws grow less. Women's lips become more plump. Their eyes look bigger. Their skin is thick and rich in collagen.

The masculine jaw becomes more square and broad, and the feminine jaw becomes smaller when more sex hormones are released.

An example of a highly feminine face is the timeless beauty, Audrey Hepburn, seen in *Figure 55*. When you place the Marquardt Beauty Mask over her face, her jaw is too small for the mask. Her oestrogen levels were so high during puberty that her nose and jaw growth were restricted.

Feminine women are always seen as more attractive by both sexes. Yet, male faces can be deemed attractive if they are more or less masculine. When women hit peak fertility in their ovulation cycle, they tend to prefer more masculine partners. At other times, they favour less masculine faces.[3]

Figure 55 – Audrey Hepburn, an ideal of female beauty.

Beauty Is Not In The Eye of the Beholder

We can accurately spot the most beautiful from the least beautiful very consistently, irrespective of cultural, racial or gender divides. There is very broad consensus in beauty. No group would ever suggest that Audrey Hepburn wasn't beautiful, for example. While different people have different taste, virtually everyone is attracted to the most beautiful in society and virtually no-one is attracted to the least attractive in society.

The *Survival Of The Fittest* Argument For Facial Development Doesn't Stand Up To Scrutiny

An obvious, but flawed, argument emerges when we talk about jaws and tooth alignment; the "survival of the fittest" argument: *Those without perfectly aligned teeth would have died young.* Or, to put it another way, *only those with perfect alignment would have survived.*

Perfectly aligned teeth require wide, forward-grown jaws. Otherwise jaws are too small and teeth become crowded. We can refute the survival of the fittest argument in two ways. Firstly, crooked teeth don't cause premature death. Orthodontists tell young children with crooked teeth that they can affix braces in a few years, and no parent, child or orthodontist fears death-by-crooked-teeth in the meantime. Children with crooked teeth who skip braces don't die from crooked teeth either.

Secondly, the skull record suggests that crooked teeth in children didn't kill in history either, as crooked teeth didn't exist. All the children's skulls in the Morton Collection have the same straight teeth as adults. George Catlin - lawyer, explorer and portrait artist - also found zero evidence of crooked teeth in children's skulls in Native Americans. He tells us, after seeing skulls in native burial grounds, *"amongst several hundreds of these skulls, I was forcibly struck with the almost incredibly small proportion of crania of children; and even more so, in the almost unexceptional completeness and soundness (and total absence of malformation) of their beautiful sets of teeth, of all ages."*[4]

Until very recently, humans - just like every other animal on earth - didn't suffer from malocclusion. Malocclusion is a disease of civilisation, just like obesity. As there is no evidence of obesity before agriculture, there is no evidence of misaligned jaws either. Jaw alignment is not genetically predetermined. As previously mentioned, Darwin didn't believe that the facial changes he witnessed (at a time when people started eating mainly cooked food at every meal - in four distinct societies) were genetically caused.

Live closer to a hunter-gatherer lifestyle, and you'll have better facial development. While society assumes that genetics is responsible for our changing jaws, the academic consensus states that two periods in history caused our faces to change; the shifts to agriculture and industrialisation.

These advancements each affected our jaws. Farming was bad. Industrialisation was worse. Each society adopted farming, then industry, at different times. These shifts cause beauty and health vulnerabilities, which affect most of us, and which can therefore be mitigated against by living more in accordance with our past in certain, specific ways. Those ways are represented by the Beauty & Health Quadrants.

If someone who has facial disproportion today was born 12,000 years ago, they would have better facial proportion by virtue of how people 12,000 years ago consumed and lived. Genes are not the primary cause of facial disproportion, environmental forces are. What we consume, how we consume, our habits, and levels of chronic inflammation shape how our faces develop. The *Beauty & Health Quadrants* reveal which elements fulfil or destroy our genetic potentials.

Where Beauty Potential Is Lost On The Face...

Your face tells the story of how healthily you breathed, ate and held yourself when you grew up. The first 18 years of life are the story of your mouth posture, your breathing efficiency, whether your diet inflamed you, how tough your food was, how much you chewed, whether your swallow adapted from an infant suckle to an adult swallow, and whether you got enough Vitamin D. The face reveals whether your environmental expectations were met. Physically, this manifests through the position of your facial bones and how your face is formed.

Upper Face
Eyes

Droopy eyebrows. The outer edge of eyebrows tend to sit higher above the eye in well developed faces. In part this is because the eyebrows are dragged down by vertical growth from the cheekbones and maxilla, and in part because muscle definition is lost when people don't chew enough.

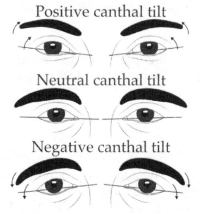

Figure 56 - Canthal tilt

Canthal Tilt is the way your eyes tilt from the inside of each eye. (See *Figure 56.*) When the maxilla grows forwards instead of down, the cheekbones grow upwards and outwards. Remember: If downwards growth is stopped, everything grows forwards and to the sides. Conversely, downward growth causes the face to melt down.

Beautiful people tend to have positive canthal tilt and high, well-projected cheekbones. The cheekbones are supported by a forward and laterally grown Maxilla. Without support, the cheekbones instead drop down the face. Then you see a negative canthal tilt. This is less beautiful as the maxilla and the cheekbones aren't as projected. Canthal tilt also raises or drags down your eyebrows.

A negative canthal tilt often combines with scleral show.

Scleral show occurs when you see the white of the eye below the iris. The Japanese call scleral show *"sanpaku"* - meaning "three whites." That's the white of the eye seen to the left, to the right, and *under* the iris. The Japanese believe that sanpaku is caused by overconsumption of drugs, alcohol, sugar and grain. When under-eye support from both the maxilla and the cheekbones is weak, both sets of bones fall down the face.

Tired Eyes refer to bags underneath the eye. Bags appear because under-eye support is weak. The area directly beneath the eyes has less support (which is also why some people have scleral show) from both the maxilla and the cheekbones. This often leads to more prominent bags.

When looking at someone side-on, you see forward growth or not. If the area under the eye falls vertically it's not forward-grown, if it's projected outwards, it is. Tired eyes are a result of a lack of under-eye projection.

Cosmetic Procedures: People try to counteract aesthetic eye deficiencies, through brow and face lifts. Some even get acid facial fillers to combat scleral show.

Cheekbones

Flat cheekbones occur when the maxilla drops downwards instead of forwards and outwards. The zygomatic bones - your cheekbones - also drop, instead of being pushed upwards and outwards. High cheekbones cause a more positive canthal tilt. Put a finger on each cheekbone and lift your finger upwards and you can mimic a positive canthal tilt. Pull downwards and you see a more negative tilt. Your canthal tilt reflects the projection of your cheekbones. Those with high, projected cheekbones are far more likely to have forward grown maxillas and shorter faces.

Cosmetic Procedures: Cheek implants cause higher-looking cheekbones.

Upper facial width

Forward and lateral growth of the Maxilla nudges the cheekbones up and out, leading to a slightly wider face. This is another sign of facial beauty. When the maxilla comes forward, the cheekbones protrude in pleasing ways, leading to high cheekbones and the potential for hollow cheeks. When the maxilla sinks down, cheekbones and everything around the eyes are negatively affected.

The Maxilla
Nose

The nose sits fully on the maxilla. It is the beginning of the airway. All of these problems are inner U problems caused by the tongue not supporting the maxilla, causing it to drop. Weaker support leads to a less attractive nose and a smaller nasal cavity. A straight nose occurs when the maxilla is projected forwards and outwards. In women, a slender nose typically goes hand-in-hand with a forward grown maxilla as higher oestrogen slims it.

Roman noses are so-called because they occurred so frequently in Ancient Rome. The Roman diet of grain-heavy foods - needed to feed the vast city-dwelling population - caused humps in the nose. For many, grain-heavy diets cause inflammation, which leads to mouth breathing and a lack of forward growth. The Romans saw Roman noses as a sign of wisdom (we'd all like to write our own reviews!) In reality, they're a sign of vertical growth and poor mouth posture.

The nasal hump occurs as the lower half of the nose lacks support from the interior nasal spine in the maxilla. The top half is supported by the nasal bone, between the eyes. The maxilla supports the bottom half. Dorsal humps form when the maxilla is too far back to offer robust support and keep the nose straight. We generally view Roman noses as unattractive. A straight nose, or a nose that protrudes upwards at the tip, is a sign of the maxilla being forward grown.

A **deviated septum** occurs when the nasal septum is not straight. It can lead to breathing issues and asymmetry. It occurs because the Maxilla doesn't offer a strong enough foundation to your nose. When the tongue and lower jaw haven't given enough support to the maxilla, it can tilt laterally. Septoplasty is the procedure that surgeons use to correct this.

Big noses, in reality, are very rare. Noses that *look* too big are due to recessed maxillas, not due to genetics. Imagine a sapling tree emerging through the soil. It's 1 inch tall. Now, if you press down the soil around it, suddenly it's 1.5 inches tall. The proper length of the sapling is 1 inch, unless you interfere with the natural order. The same principle applies to noses. Noses that appear big, do so because the maxilla is too far back (like pressing down soil around a sapling tree), not because the nose is intrinsically too big. Take a 'big' nose and then move the upper jaw 1cm more forwards and you will see that maxillary position defines the perception of nose size.

Men have bigger noses than women - by about 10% - as men have more muscle mass which requires more air. This further highlights why only women who are very efficient and devoid of inflammation get the full dose of oestrogen at puberty, as oestrogen slims female noses considerably.

Droopy nose. Some people find that the tip of their nose droops downwards. This is because the Maxilla is too far back to offer adequate support. Therefore, the nose droops down. This commonly occurs with Roman noses.

Cosmetic Procedures: Rhinoplasty - a nose job - is the most common cosmetic surgery. It straightens and slims down noses. Many people believe their nose is too far forwards for their face. In reality, their jaws are set too far back to offer adequate support. Nose jobs trick our brains to believe we are seeing forward growth and, in women, high oestrogen levels.

Nasolabial folds

Nasolabial folds are the indentation that runs from the base of the nose to the corners of the mouth. They are always present when you smile or laugh. However, they can appear on a resting face too. They become more pronounced as we age. The underlying cause is that the maxilla dropped too far back, due to improper mouth posture.

Long philtrum

The philtrum is the indentation or groove from the base of the nasal septum to the upper lip. In beautiful people, the philtrum tends to be short. When the maxilla drops, the philtrum can extend. All babies have very short philtrums. Philtrums become longer when vertical growth occurs and the body is forced to compensate.

Mouth

The mouth is a key area for beauty and health. It's vital for the two smaller layers of the *Hierarchy of Survival*; drinking and eating. For some, it is used for breathing too, at high aesthetic cost. The mouth also plays a role in how healthy we sound. Physically-caused speech impediments occur when jaws are misaligned, or the mouth is too small.

Thin lips: Lips are seen as a vital part of beauty. One of the most popular non-surgical cosmetic procedures is having lip fillers. There is a remarkably good reason for this, and it's not because the patients lips are naturally too small. Instead, it's because the Maxilla and Mandible don't project forwards enough. Lip fillers, like nose jobs, imitate large airways and forward-grown jaws.

When both jaws are recessed, you will have thin lips. A forward-grown upper jaw but recessed lower jaw leads to a fuller upper lip and a thinner lower lip. A recessed upper jaw and a forward-grown lower jaw leads to a thinner upper lip and fuller lower lip. When you have a perfectly projected face, both lips will be full and at a top-to-bottom lip ratio of 1:1.618. In females, better facial development leads to increased oestrogen, which plumps up the lips even more.

Here's a little test to prove that jaw projection affects lip size: Keep your lips sealed and move air into the space between your teeth and your closed lips. This will puff up your lips and they appear bigger. This mimics forward-grown jaws. When your jaws aren't forward grown enough, more of the lips are inside your mouth. When your jaws are very forward grown, more of your lips show outside, making them look bigger. If everyone had very forward grown faces, lip fillers would be less popular.

Narrow mouth (narrow dental arch): We can spot a narrow maxilla by observing a narrow dental arch. The distance between the molar teeth reveals how wide your upper jaw is. This is the maxilla's base. A wide dental arch is best seen when someone smiles and you see a mouth full of teeth. Smaller mouths are a sign of a narrow and recessed dental arch. The ratio of the width of the base of the nose to the width of the mouth should be 1:1.618. This ratio is corrupted when you have a narrow dental arch.

When the dental arch grows wide, there is more room for teeth. (See *Figure 57, overleaf.*) Also, the base of your nasal cavity is wider, the maxilla is wider, making your cheekbones push out wider, making your canthal tilt more positive. The width of the mouth is wider too.

The dental arch is shaped by proper tongue placement on the roof of the mouth. Narrow dental arches occur when the tongue is absent, and doesn't guide the upper teeth outwards. Your inter-molar width should be as wide as your tongue. A tongue that drops down in the mouth causes improper development of your teeth and your maxilla, leaving you with a narrow and recessed dental arch and maxilla, and crooked teeth.

Figure 57 - Margot Robbie has a large mouth and a wide dental arch.

Sunken Mouth: A recessed maxilla leaves the mouth sunken too far back in the head. This is why we can look at someone - full face on - with seemingly good facial proportions, yet they are deemed unattractive. They have a strong outer U and a weak inner U. A recessed mouth leads to the airway and nasal cavity being smaller than they should be.

Vaulted Palate: When the roof of your mouth is high and narrow, like the roof of an old English church, you have a vaulted palate. It often goes hand-in-hand with narrow dental arches and crooked teeth. The maxilla doesn't grow properly, either forwards or laterally, and instead drops down. This is due to the complete absence of tongue support. When mouth posture is wrong, everything can go wrong.

Some develop so poorly that their tongue doesn't fit onto the roof of their mouth. The roof of your mouth is where your tongue belongs *always*, except when talking and eating. You can tell when people have always had good mouth posture because their dental arch has been shaped by their tongue. Their dental arch will be wide and their maxilla will be forward-grown. When the tongue doesn't offer support, the mouth, and the whole face collapses and lengthens, and the palate is vaulted. (See *Figure 58, overleaf.*)

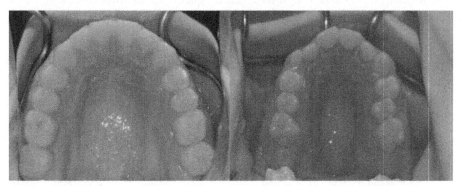

Figure 58 - A normal palare (left) and a vaulted palate (right).

Crooked Teeth: Crooked teeth are caused by poor mouth posture - including tongue position and lip seal at rest - mouth breathing and not chewing enough tough food. These environmental expectations were met in virtually all of our distant ancestors. Their skulls reveal perfectly straight teeth and no malocclusion.

Tooth tipping is the other element to consider. Tongue position at rest and lip seal at rest also define whether your teeth tip. Tongue position pushes teeth out. Lip seal pushes teeth in. When they are in harmony, the teeth don't tip inwards or outwards.

The Lower Jaw (Mandible)

The mandible – part of the outer U – also affects beauty and airway size. When the mandible is recessed, it's also frequently too narrow, and instead of forward growth, you get downward growth. If it protrudes - as it does with people who have an underbite - it also grows downwards. All of these issues are manifested by how you breathe, where your tongue rests in your mouth, whether your lower teeth are in contact with your upper teeth at rest, and how much you chew tough food.

Narrow Jaw: We are attracted to vertically short, horizontally wide faces. The two reasons for a narrow jaw are; downward growth, where the bone remodels downwards; and lack of strong masseter (chewing) muscles. The lower jaw develops best when you chew lots of tough food and when your mouth posture is correct. If either of these are not done enough, your jaw growth will be compromised.

Recessed Jaw: Generally, both modern upper and lower jaws are set back in the face, leaving a tiny airway and an unattractive face. This is so common in Western societies that it is seen as normal. Recessed jaws lead to breathing issues - such as snoring and sleep apnea - and vertical growth.

Protruding Jaw: Some people have a protruding lower jaw and an underbite. This is defined by the position of the tongue at rest. When the tongue rests in the lower jaw, it guides lower jaw growth abnormally and inhibits upper jaw growth.

Pointy Chin: Often, when people have recessed jaws, the chin is pointy (and vertically long.) Pointy chins occur because the lower front teeth are set back further than they should be. This is a byproduct of the lower teeth following the upper teeth backwards. If the upper jaw is recessed, the teeth in your lower jaw will fall back too, but the chin still protrudes like a witch's chin.

Age-Related Facial Issues

As we age, issues with facial development become more obvious. We see lines and wrinkles. We also see fat dropping down the face. Here are a few issues that affect those who have improper facial development.

Older people can get double chins and jowls. Double chins occur far more in people with recessed lower jaws than others. They also occur in people with incorrect mouth posture. Jowls are a sign of improper swallowing (leading to fat in cheeks, instead of hollow cheeks) which then drops down the face with age. If you are overweight, these issues compound.

Marionette lines are the lines from the sides of your lips down your chin. This occurs when people have fat cheeks (rather than hollow cheeks from proper swallowing) and a lack of forward growth. These lines occur far more in people who mouth breathe.

People with forward-grown faces look younger than others who lack forward growth. Correct mouth posture and correct swallowing are preventative measures against double chins and jowls. Correct mouth posture means that the submental space - where double chins form - is tense. Correct swallowing means that buccal fat and muscle on the cheeks is lost, so there is less sagging in later life. Hollow cheeks are hollow due to high cheekbones and a lack of fat or muscle in the cheeks. Losing weight helps with these age-related issues.

Why Traditional Dentists Are Winning

There is a war between traditional dentists and Orthotropics, that dentists are winning. Since the 1960s, orthodontists have set their remit as straightening teeth. That's it. They do this successfully, but dentists don't see that crooked or crowded teeth are just a symptom of facial development issues. In straightening teeth, and pulling them backwards, dentists damage faces.

In its infancy, Dr. Edward Angle, the founder of modern orthodontics, believed that all 32 teeth should be preserved in the mouth. His favourite student, Dr. Charles Tweed, believed that extractions were favourable. Tweed's philosophy has lingered up until today, at the costs of flatter, narrower faces, jaw joint problems, neck pain and migraines, smaller dental arches, bone loss from the jaws of teeth that have been extracted, jaw recession, a narrower upper airway, and far less attractive faces.

We go to dentists, and they say, *"Your upper teeth are crowded. We can fix that with braces. And you have impacted wisdom teeth. It's best to remove them before they cause issues."* They don't say, your jaws are recessed because you habitually mouth breathe. They don't consider facial harmony. Sometimes they remove 4 teeth from the upper dental arch to make room to straighten the rest by pulling them backwards.

Figure 59 is the profile outline of a boy whose face didn't develop properly, before (left) and after fixed braces and extractions (right). His jaws become more recessed, his nose appears much bigger, his lips are thinner. His face is longer and less attractive.

Figure 59 – Profile outline of a boy who had braces and extractions. Before (left) and after (right).

Twin studies reveal the damage that traditional orthodontics can do.

Figure 60 – Twins where one twin (left) had extractions and the other twin (right) did not, and had her palate expanded.

Both twins – see *Figure 60* - had dental work. The twin on the right had no extractions and had a palate expander which expands intermolar width, just like a properly positioned tongue. The twin on the left had extractions and fixed braces. The left face is longer and narrower. This is the danger of having tooth extractions, and it should be stopped.

Another case where one twin decided against any dental work and the other opted for extractions and braces highlights the point – *Figure 61*.

Figure 61 – One twin (top row) declined orthodontics. The other (bottom row) had treatment.

No one goes to a dentist to look uglier. But that is what happens. When the lips are sealed and you can't see someone's teeth, most of the time their before-treatment face was better looking than their after-treatment face.

Go to a dentist with crowded, crooked or impacted teeth, and they only focus on straightening the teeth. Fixed braces pull the teeth back into the mouth, recessing the jaws further. Dentists often remove teeth to make space before straightening them. This reduces the length and width of the dental arches. Teeth become straighter and faces become uglier. Younger faces and softer bones are more adversely affected by fixed braces. The beauty bones – the maxilla, cheekbones, and lower jaw – are pulled backwards. This is a disaster for beauty.

Dentists attack Orthotropics because the results of Orthotropics are inconsistent and the results of orthodontics are very consistent. When you don't address the inflammation problem or change habits, faces grow wrongly.

For dentists, it's a slam dunk case. They always deliver what they intend to, because fixed braces always straighten teeth. But when the cost is beauty, their remit is flawed. Orthotropic failures can be blamed on non-compliance. (See *Figure 62*.) The failed children didn't manage to keep their mouths closed.

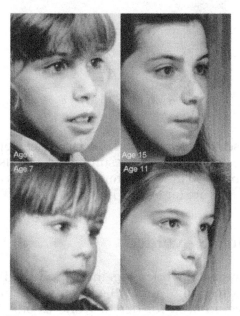

Figure 62 – The sister (top row) who couldn't keep her mouth shut had poor results. The sister who kept her mouth shut (bottom row) had ideal results.

If dentistry and Orthotropics were cancer drugs, dentistry would be approved and Orthotropics would not. Something must successfully treat everyone for it to gain prominence. However, in the same way that chemotherapy does long-term damage to patients, orthodontics does too.

Yet, in choosing orthodontics over Orthotropics, we are choosing to damage facial harmony. This can be seen when we compare a twin who underwent orthodontic treatment and compare him with his brother who had successful orthotropic treatment.

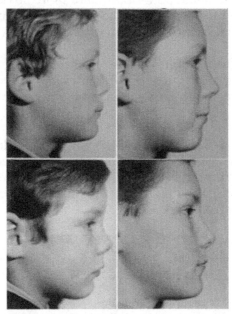

Figure 63 – Orthodontic results (top row) versus orthotropic results (bottom row) in twins.

In *Figure 63*, we see the twin with worse facial development at 8 years old (bottom row) had a far better result because he used orthotropics, not extractions and fixed braces. Before treatment, his case was slightly worse, but his results are far better. The impact of orthodontics is clear.

Dentistry Can Be Avoided...

To avoid needing dental work altogether, apply the Beauty Quadrant from birth. Children who apply the Beauty Quadrant from birth, consistently, have no need for dental work, as our distant ancestors show us.

Myofunctional therapy is based on the Beauty Quadrant, highlighting again that experts understand that people develop wrongly due to posture and function. This book was written to make the knowledge you've just read mainstream.

Your Next Steps...

Beauty potential and health potential are our birthrights. When we fulfil our environmental expectations, we turn those potentials into reality. Beauty potential doesn't slip away in those with an optimal Beauty Quadrant. We have seen how consumption defines both beauty and health. How we breathe, swallow and eat directly define facial development. Nose breathers who maintain natural mouth posture - whenever they aren't eating or talking - develop beautifully. A fully developed adult swallow maintains beauty potential; where upper and lower teeth touch, lips are together, and the tongue presses hard against the palate. Those who chew and break down tough food with their jaws retain their beauty. More beauty potential would be retained if we also chose to eat the toughest of foods with hand and tooth, instead of relying of knives, forks or chopsticks.

Sitting and standing tall and straight, while keeping the head in perfect alignment when we aren't communicating retains our beauty potential too. We must beware the dangers of lazy posture, in our bodies and our faces.

Maintaining the Beauty Quadrant would have been far easier in our pre-agrarian past, when our environmental expectations weren't compromised by heated homes, TV dinners or a daily commute engaging with traffic or smart phones. The Beauty Quadrant is not commonly maintained in the present world. It's also, unfortunately, time limited. We only have so much opportunity to shape and direct our facial bones and their sutures before 15 years are up.

Every parent has a duty to ensure that their child grows as naturally and healthily as possible. This encompasses both the Beauty Quadrant and the Health Quadrant. The duty starts at birth. If a baby has an open mouth, their parent should gently close it, every single time. Allowing bad habits to form can decrease beauty, health and cognition. Breastfeeding is far superior to bottle-feeding, in terms of the Beauty Quadrant, because it takes natural effort. It is also custom-made, natural milk for a baby. Its properties change based on the environment. It enhances the Health Quadrant as much as the Beauty Quadrant, in most cases.

Young children are averse to using cutlery. They are far more engaged in eating when they are in control. Let them pick up food with their hands, and attempt to break it down themselves. Give them vegetables, meat, fish and fruit. They will naturally pick what is best for them, provided it's natural and unprocessed. As a child, the things I hated - but was forced - to eat were the things I later learned I had intolerances to. In this sense, a parent doesn't know best!

If a young child has so much mucus in their nose that maintaining natural mouth posture is impossible, forcing them to mouth breathe, there are two steps to take. The first is immediate; unblocking the nose. The second is to turn detective and figure out which foods caused inflammation. Banning grains, sugar and dairy is a good first step. Children are better off eating tough meat than the soft vegetables that parents believe are best for their development. Let their jaws ache when they chew. It's the natural way.

Parents should teach their children how to maintain natural mouth posture, how to swallow (if they see swallowing go awry) and how to break down tough foods. Body posture should also be taught. All of these should be enforced every time you see your child slip up.

Older people should chew hard gum. We can all encourage our bodies to be strong in natural, fundamental ways, and jaw strength is beneficial to anyone, of any age. It helps keep the mouth shut, to maintain natural mouth posture, and to breathe naturally.

The Health Quadrant is imperative for far longer than 15 years. It spans our lifetime. It defines our health-span; the amount of our lives where we retain good health. It's a powerful ally of our Beauty Quadrant when it's strong. It acts as a potent enemy to the Beauty Quadrant and our everyday lives when it's weak.

A weak Health Quadrant will corrupt a strong Beauty Quadrant in many ways. It will make us mouth breathe when we sleep. It will block our nose when we are inflamed. It affects natural mouth posture and natural body posture. And the implications of this in the first 15 years of life are not trivial. When a weak Health Quadrant causes the face to develop wrongly, the nasal cavity grows smaller, the upper airway has bottlenecks, the jaws recess and our whole lives are negatively affected.

Ensuring that Health Quadrants thrive is not just a duty for a parent, but a duty as a person. A duty to yourself. First, we must optimise breathing. Natural mouth posture and efficient breathing go hand-in-hand. They form a virtuous circle. Healthy, efficient, low-volume breathing accommodates uninterrupted nose breathing and natural mouth posture.

Breathing is affected by mouth posture, what we eat and when, exercise and Vitamin D levels. It's also affected by breathing exercises and using a breathing device which elevates our CO_2 tolerance. Breathing either supports or insults our immune system.

Food is a huge contributor to inflammation; both it terms of what we eat and when we eat. Repairing the gut barrier is a key concern. We should be alert to inflammation. It could be caused by any ingredient that we have eaten recently. The constant barrage of inflammatory foods passing through the gut wall can cause long-term damage in virtually any part of the human body.

Cutting out grains - especially gluten-filled wheat, rye & barley - sugar, and dairy is enough for many people to repair their gut. For those who are chronically inflamed, take a food intolerance test, or start an elimination diet. You can speed up your understanding by having an inflammation blood test, or a skin prick/patch test. The skin prick or patch test indicates how you react to potential allergens on the skin.

Some intolerances and allergies will forever remain unresolved. But, the immune system can "forget" certain insults with time and avoidance of them. When the gut is repaired and you don't eat things to tear it open again, you'll have far better control over your inflammatory triggers.

Exercise and Vitamin D possess anti-inflammatory effects. Fifteen minutes of sun exposure and fifteen minutes of exercise - which can be completed at the same time - can enhance your immunity. This will improve your appearance and your health. All four elements of the Health Quadrant improve quality of life and health-span.

Cheats To Improve Your Potentials

We can elevate our Health Quadrant with the following purchases. They aren't needed, but the speed up the process of fortifying your Health Quadrant significantly.

> Beauty Potential Breathing Device
> Vitamin D supplement & Vitamin D tests
> Mastic Gum
> Mouth tape
> A food & inflammation tracking app

The Beauty Potential Breathing Device teaches your body to quickly cope with higher concentrations of CO_2. This dramatically reduces breathing volume. When you feel less air hunger, breathing slows. I recommend using a breathing device daily.

Vitamin D supplements are a safe and effective way to increase your Vitamin D levels without exposing yourself to dangerous levels of sunshine. We are supposed to be exposed to the sun. Its beams, in the right quantities, help us. This is typically why many people look healthier after going on vacation. We should try to get direct sunlight for 15-30 minutes every day. Vitamin D supplements will bump up your levels alongside this sun exposure. You can also take Vitamin D tests to see what your Vitamin D levels are.

Mastic gum is the world's hardest gum. It should be chewed daily. When you start chewing it, you should only do it for a few minutes a day. This should rise, over 3-6 months, until you are chewing for 30-60 minutes per day.

Mouth tape should be applied vertically on your lips when you go to sleep. It stops mouth breathing when you are unconscious. We spend a third of our lives sleeping, and ensuring that those 8 hours aren't spent mouth breathing increases your health, your breathing efficiency, and your levels of inflammation.

A **food & inflammation tracking app** will illuminate what foods may be problematic for you, so you can stop eating them and improve your Health Quadrant. Unfortunately, in today's world, chronic inflammation is seen as a part of life. However, it's very detrimental to both health and beauty. Stopping chronic inflammation has no downsides, in the way that quitting smoking has no downsides. You may be giving up something you love, but there are zero negative consequences for your body.

All these products are available on my website at tcarneybowles.com. Most of them are available from other places too. Feel free to shop around or get the products that I recommend at my store.

Rules of Beauty Potentials

Shut your mouth: Teeth touching, lips sealed and tongue held against your upper palate.

Chew lots of tough foods: Chew every mouthful more than 20 times until food is liquified. Eat big slabs of meat with your hands.

Swallow Properly: Seal your lips, make your teeth touch, pause for a moment, then swallow with your tongue touching your palate hard from the front to the back, *slowly*.

Stand & Sit Tall: Maintain a straight back, make sure your head is straight and looking forwards.

Rules of Health Potentials

Breathing: Breathe lightly. When you are breathing so lightly saliva forms in your mouth, your body is in relaxed. Always breathe through the nose. Do breathing exercises to improve your CO_2 tolerance. Use a Beauty Potential Breathing Device if you want faster, more effective results.

What To Eat: If you have signs of inflammation, get tested or go on a strict elimination diet. Your goal is to find out what is causing your inflammation. You can slowly add foods back into your diet one at a time to see if your immune system is triggered by an insult. A skin prick test or a blood test can be used if you don't want to restrict your diet.

When To Eat: Having eating windows, such as a 6 hour feeding window and 18 hours of fasting, does wonders for your immune system, weight and general health.

Exercise: Physical exercise is an immune-building weapon that also improves your mental and physical well-being. When you combine it with breathing exercises, you easily fortify your Health Quadrant.

Vitamin D: Brief, daily exposure to direct sunlight strengthens your immune system. I recommend a daily dose and supplementation to vastly increase your Vitamin D levels. Blood tests show you how deficient you are and allow you to control your dose of Vitamin D supplements.

If you'd like more information, or to get some of the tests and products I've mentioned, visit my website. I have a newsletter and you'll be the first to get access to new books in the series. Visit it now and sign up at http://tcarneybowles.com

Acknowledgements

I'd like to thank my partner, Vlada, for bearing with me as I wrote (and rewrote) this book. Sasha, for keeping me smiling.

I'd also like to thank Paul R. Ehrlich and Sandra Kahn for their help. I recommend that you read their book, *Jaws: The Story of a Hidden Epidemic*. And thank you to John Mew, for being so helpful, laying the groundwork, and allowing me to reproduce his images. His book, *The Cause and Cure of Malocclusion*, is a must read for people interested in this topic.

Thanks to Arturo Aguirre for your artwork and professionalism.

To all my family, for their love and support in life. And the Grinners, you know who you are.

References

Beauty Quadrant I: Mouth Posture

1 Hsu, E., Andiappan, M., & Yow, M. (2019). The effect of tongue pressure on maxillary arch width. Progress in Orthodontics, 20(1), 26. https://doi.org/10.1186/s40510-019-0278-9

Beauty Quadrant II: How To Eat

[1] Wilson, B. (2013). Consider the fork: A history of how we cook and eat. Basic Books.

[2] Marx, K. (1939). Grundrisse [Outlines of the critique of political economy]. Penguin Books.

[3] Heikkinen, E. V., Vuollo, V., Harila, V., Sidlauskas, A., & Heikkinen, T. (2022). Facial asymmetry and chewing sides in twins. Acta Odontologica Scandinavica, 80(3), 197-202. https://doi.org/10.1080/00016357.2021.1985166

Beauty Quadrant IV: Body Posture

[1] Solow, B., & Sandham, A. (2002). Cranio-cervical posture: a factor in the development and function of the dentofacial structures. European Journal of Orthodontics, 24(5), 441-456. https://doi.org/10.1093/ejo/24.5.441

Health Quadrant II: What to Eat

[1] Lennerz, B. S., Mey, J. T., Henn, O. H., & Ludwig, D. S. (2021). Behavioral Characteristics and Self-Reported Health Status among 2029 Adults Consuming a "Carnivore Diet". Current Developments in Nutrition, 5(12), nzab133. https://doi.org/10.1093/cdn/nzab133

Health Quadrant III: Exercise

[1] McDougall, C. (2009). Born to run (Chapter 27, pp. 212-222). Knopf Doubleday Publishing Group.

[2] Groom, D. (1971). Cardiovascular observations on Tarahumara Indian runners—the modern Spartans. American Heart Journal, 81(3), 304-314. https://doi.org/10.1016/0002-8703(71)90099-8

[3] Ibid.

Facial Development In History

[1] Brennan, W. (2020, August 20). How Two British Orthodontists Became Celebrities to Incels. The New York Times Magazine. https://www.nytimes.com/2020/08/20/magazine/teeth-mewing-incels.html

[2] English, T. (2020, January 27). Could old skulls help us understand why we have crooked teeth? WHYY. https://whyy.org/segments/could-old-skulls-help-us-understand-why-we-have-crooked-teeth/

[3] Shifting Faces Over 10,000 Years. (2005). World Archaeology, 14. https://www.world-archaeology.com/issues/issue-14/changing-faces-over-ten-millennia

[4] Kahn, S., & Ehrlich, P. R. (2018). Jaws: The Story of a Hidden Epidemic (p. 9). Stanford University Press.

[5] Lieberman, D. (2013). The Story of the Human Body: Evolution, Health and Disease. Penguin UK.

[6] Begg, P. R. (1954). Stone age man's dentition: With reference to anatomically correct occlusion, the etiology of malocclusion, and a technique for its treatment. American Journal of Orthodontics, 40(4), 298-312. https://doi.org/10.1016/0002-9416(54)90092-5

[7] Waugh, L. M. (1937). Influence of Diet on the Jaws and Face of the American Eskimo. The Journal of the American Dental Association and The Dental Cosmos, 24(10), 1640–1647. https://doi.org/10.14219/jada.archive.1937.0295

[8] Wood, B. F. (1971). Malocclusion in the modern Alaskan Eskimo. American Journal of Orthodontics, 60(4), 344-354. https://doi.org/10.1016/0002-9416(71)90147-3

[9] Corruccini, R. S., & Lee, G. T. R. (1984). Occlusal variation in Chinese immigrants to the United Kingdom and their offspring. Archives of Oral Biology, 29(10), 779-782. https://doi.org/10.1016/0003-9969(84)90006-2

Beauty Quadrant I: Mouth Posture (Further Reading)

[1] Niemcewicz, J. U. (1965). Under Their Vine and Fig Tree. Travels Through America in 1797-1799, 1805 With Some Further Account of Life in New Jersey (p. 31). Grassman Publishing Co.

[2] Catlin, G. (1870). Shut Your Mouth... and Save Your Life (4th ed., p. 17). N. Truebner and Co. (Reprinted by Kessinger Publishing, Whitefish, MT).

[3] Catlin, G. (1870). Shut Your Mouth... and Save Your Life (4th ed., p. 13). N. Truebner and Co. (Reprinted by Kessinger Publishing, Whitefish, MT).

[4] Catlin, G. (1870). Shut Your Mouth... and Save Your Life (4th ed.). N. Truebner and Co. (Reprinted by Kessinger Publishing, Whitefish, MT).

[5] Ibid.

[6] Ibid.

[7] Ibid.

[8] Malhotra, S., Pandey, R. K., Nagar, A., Agarwal, S. P., & Gupta, V. K. (2012). The effect of mouth breathing on dentofacial morphology of growing child. Journal of Indian Society of Pedodontics and Preventive Dentistry, 30(1), 27-31. https://doi.org/10.4103/0970-4388.95572

[9] Bresolin, D., Shapiro, P. A., Shapiro, G. G., Chapko, M. K., & Dassel, S. (1983). Mouth breathing in allergic children: Its relationship to dentofacial development. American Journal of Orthodontics, 83(4), 334-340. https://doi.org/10.1016/0002-9416(83)90229-4

[10] Harari, D., Redlich, M., Miri, S., Hamud, T., & Gross, M. (2010). The effect of mouth breathing versus nasal breathing on dentofacial and craniofacial development in orthodontic patients. The Laryngoscope, 120(10), 2089-2093. https://doi.org/10.1002/lary.20991

[11] Behlfelt, K., Linder-Aronson, S., McWilliam, J., Neander, P., & Laage-Hellman, J. (1990). Cranio-facial morphology in children with and without enlarged tonsils. European Journal of Orthodontics, 12(3), 233-243. https://doi.org/10.1093/ejo/12.3.233

[12] Yu, M., & Gao, X. (2019). Tongue pressure distribution of individual normal occlusions and exploration of related factors. Journal of Oral Rehabilitation, 46(3), 249-256. https://doi.org/10.1111/joor.12741

Beauty Quadrant II: How To Eat... (Further Reading)

[1] Ferrie, H. (1997). An interview with C. Loring Brace. Current Anthropology, 38(5), 862. https://doi.org/10.1086/204678

[2] Caesar, J. (55-54 BCE). The Gallic Wars (Book 5, Chapter 14).

[3] Primitive Form of the Skull [Review of the article 'On the Primitive Form of the Skull']. (1868, October). Anthropological Review, 6(23), 426.

[4] Darwin, C. (1871). The Descent of Man, and Selection in Relation to Sex (Vol. 1). John Murray.

[5] Ingervall, B., & Thilander, B. (1974). Relation between facial morphology and activity of the masticatory muscles. Journal of Oral Rehabilitation, 1(2), 131-147. https://doi.org/10.1111/j.1365-2842.1974.tb00771.x

[6] Ingervall, B., & Helkimo, E. (1978). Masticatory muscle force and facial morphology in man. Archives of Oral Biology, 23(3), 203-206. https://doi.org/10.1016/0003-9969(78)90191-3

[7] Ortensi, L., Martini, M., Montanari, M., Lavazzini, M. C., & Ortensi, A. (2017). A Simplified method to identify patient face type for a prosthodontic treatment plan. Journal of Dental Health, Oral Disorders & Therapy, 8(4), 553-556. https://doi.org/10.15406/jdhodt.2017.08.00291

[8] Ibid.

[9] Heikkinen, E. V., Vuollo, V., Harila, V., Sidlauskas, A., & Heikkinen, T. (2022). Facial asymmetry and chewing sides in twins. Acta Odontologica Scandinavica, 80(3), 197-202. https://doi.org/10.1080/00016357.2021.1985166

Beauty Quadrant III: Swallowing (Further Reading)

[1] World Health Organization. (2011, January 15). Exclusive breastfeeding for six months best for babies everywhere. https://www.who.int/news/item/15-01-2011-exclusive-breastfeeding-for-six-months-best-for-babies-everywhere

How The Face Grows

[1] Severt, T. R., & Proffit, W. R. (1997). The prevalence of facial asymmetry in the dentofacial deformities population at the University of North Carolina. International Journal of Adult Orthodontics and Orthognathic Surgery, 12(3), 171-176.

[2] Warren, J. J., Bishara, S. E., Steinbock, K. L., Yonezu, T., & Nowak, A. J. (2001). Effects of oral habits' duration on dental characteristics in the primary dentition. The Journal of the American Dental Association, 132(12), 1685-1693. https://doi.org/10.14219/jada.archive.2001.0121

Part II: The Health Quadrant: Chronic Inflammation

[1] Brennan, W. (2020, August 20). How Two British Orthodontists Became Celebrities to Incels. The New York Times Magazine.

[2] Ibid.

[3] Corrao, G., Corazza, G. R., Bagnardi, V., Brusco, G., Ciacci, C., Cottone, M., Chambers, D., Usai, P., & Gasbarrini, G. (2001). Mortality in patients with coeliac disease and their relatives: A cohort study. Lancet, 358(9279), 356-361. https://doi.org/10.1016/S0140-6736(01)05554-4

[4] Lum, L. C. (1975). Hyperventilation: the tip and the iceberg. Journal of Psychosomatic Research, 19(5-6), 375-383. https://doi.org/10.1016/0022-3999(75)90017-3

[5] Furman, D., Hejblum, B. P., Simon, N., Jojic, V., Dekker, C. L., Thiébaut, R., Tibshirani, R. J., & Davis, M. M. (2014). Systems analysis of sex differences reveals an immunosuppressive role for testosterone in the response to influenza vaccination. Proceedings of the National Academy of Sciences of the United States of America, 111(2), 869-874. https://doi.org/10.1073/pnas.1321060111

[6] Doull, I. J. M. (2004). The effect of asthma and its treatment on growth. Archives of Disease in Childhood, 89(1), 60-63. https://doi.org/10.1136/adc.2003.014365

Health Quadrant I: Breathing (Further Reading)

[1] McKeown, P. (2015). The Oxygen Advantage: The simple, scientifically proven breathing technique that will revolutionise your health and fitness. Piatkus. Chapter 4.

[2] Studies show that an asthmatic has a breathing volume per minute of 12 to 15 liters. (McFadden & Lyons 1968, Johnson et al 1995, Bowler 1998)

[3] Rakhimov, A. (2014). Normal Breathing: The Key to Vital Health (Buteyko Method) (Vol. 4). Author.

Health Quadrant II: What to Eat (Further Reading)

[1] Hollon, J., Puppa, E. L., Greenwald, B., Goldberg, E., Guerrerio, A., & Fasano, A. (2015). Effect of gliadin on permeability of intestinal biopsy explants from celiac disease patients and patients with non-celiac gluten sensitivity. Nutrients, 7(3), 1565-1576. https://doi.org/10.3390/nu7031565

[2] Febbraio, M. A., & Karin, M. (2021). "Sweet death": Fructose as a metabolic toxin that targets the gut-liver axis. Cell Metabolism, 33(12), 2316-2328. https://doi.org/10.1016/j.cmet.2021.09.004

[3] Storhaug, C. L., Fosse, S. K., & Fadnes, L. T. (2017). Country, regional, and global estimates for lactose malabsorption in adults: a systematic review and meta-analysis. The Lancet Gastroenterology & Hepatology, 2(10), 738-746. https://doi.org/10.1016/S2468-1253(17)30154-1

Health Quadrant II (Continued): When To Eat (Further Reading)

[1] Winterman, D. (2012, November 15). Breakfast, lunch and dinner: Have we always eaten them? BBC News Magazine. https://www.bbc.co.uk/news/magazine-20243692

[2] Lawrence, F. (2008). Eat your heart out: Why the food business is bad for the planet and your health. Penguin.

[3] Carroll, A. (2013). Three squares: The invention of the American meal (Illustrated ed.). Basic Books.

[4] Kerndt, P. R., Naughton, J. L., Driscoll, C. E., & Loxterkamp, D. A. (1982). Fasting: the history, pathophysiology and complications. Western Journal of Medicine, 137(5), 379-399.

Health Quadrant IV: Vitamin D (Further Reading)

[1] Harvard Health Publishing. (2021, September 13). Vitamin D and your health: Breaking old rules, raising new hopes. Harvard Medical School. https://www.health.harvard.edu/staying-healthy/vitamin-d-and-your-health-breaking-old-rules-raising-new-hopes

[2] Levis, S., Gomez, A., Jimenez, C., Veras, L., Ma, F., Lai, S., Hollis, B., & Roos, B. A. (2005). Vitamin D deficiency and seasonal variation in an adult South Florida population. The Journal of Clinical Endocrinology & Metabolism, 90(3), 1557-1562. https://doi.org/10.1210/jc.2004-0746

[3] Czarnecki, D., Meehan, C., & Bruce, F. (2009). The vitamin D status of Australian dermatologists. Clinical and Experimental Dermatology, 34, 624-625. https://doi.org/10.1111/j.1365-2230.2008.03002.x

[4] Jolliffe, D. A., Griffiths, C. J., & Martineau, A. R. (2013). Vitamin D in the prevention of acute respiratory infection: systematic review of clinical studies. Journal of Steroid Biochemistry and Molecular Biology, 136, 321-329. https://doi.org/10.1016/j.jsbmb.2012.11.017

Beauty Is Contagious - The Theory of Propinquity

[1] Thorndike, E. L. (1920). A constant error in psychological ratings. Journal of Applied Psychology, 4(1), 25-29. https://doi.org/10.1037/h0071663

[2] Wilson, R. K., & Eckel, C. C. (2006). Judging a book by its cover: Beauty and expectations in the trust game. Political Research Quarterly, 59(2), 189-202. https://doi.org/10.1177/106591290605900202

[3] Cordain, L., Miller, J. B., Eaton, S. B., Mann, N., Holt, S. H., & Speth, J. D. (2000). Plant-animal subsistence ratios and macronutrient energy estimations in worldwide hunter-gatherer diets. American Journal of Clinical Nutrition, 71(3), 682-692. https://doi.org/10.1093/ajcn/71.3.682

[4] Wilson, R. K., & Eckel, C. C. (2006). Judging a book by its cover: Beauty and expectations in a trust game. Political Research Quarterly, 59(2), 189-202. https://doi.org/10.1177/106591290605900202

[5] Slater, A., Bremner, G., Johnson, S. P., Sherwood, P., Hayes, R., & Brown, E. (2000). Newborn infants' preference for attractive faces: The role of internal and external facial features. Infancy, 1(2), 265-274. https://doi.org/10.1207/S15327078IN0102_8

[6] Dallam, G., McClaran, S., Cox, D., & Foust, C. (2018). Effect of nasal versus oral breathing on Vo2max and physiological economy in recreational runners following an extended period spent using nasally restricted breathing. International Journal of Kinesiology and Sports Science, 6, 22-29. https://doi.org/10.7575/aiac.ijkss.v.6n.2p.22

[7] Kanazawa, S. (2011). Intelligence and physical attractiveness. Intelligence, 39(1), 7-14. https://doi.org/10.1016/j.intell.2010.11.003

[8] Childhood sleep apnea linked to brain damage, lower IQ. (2006, August 21). Johns Hopkins Medicine Media Relations and Public Affairs. https://www.hopkinsmedicine.org/Press_releases/2006/08_21_06.html

[9] Nedelec, J. L., & Beaver, K. M. (2014). Physical attractiveness as a phenotypic marker of health: An assessment using a nationally representative sample of American adults. Evolution and Human Behavior, 35(6), 456-463.

[10] Henderson, J. J., & Anglin, J. M. (2003). Facial attractiveness predicts longevity. Evolution and Human Behavior, 24(5), 351-356. https://doi.org/10.1016/S1090-5138(03)00036-9

[11] Čukić, I., Brett, C. E., Kribel, K. E., Kalziqi, A., Huber, B. R., & DeSantis, L. R. G. (2017). Childhood intelligence in relation to major causes of death in 68 year follow-up: Prospective population study. BMJ, 357, Article j2708. https://doi.org/10.1136/bmj.j2708

[12] Efran, M. G. (1974). The effect of physical appearance on the judgment of guilt, interpersonal attraction, and severity of recommended punishment in a simulated jury task. Journal of Research in Personality, 8, 45-54.

The Corruption Of The Health Quadrant

[1] Price, W. A. (1939). Chapter 7. In Nutrition and Physical Degeneration. Price-Pottenger Nutrition Foundation.

[2] Price, W. A. (1939). Chapter 21. In Nutrition and Physical Degeneration. Price-Pottenger Nutrition Foundation.

[3] Ibid.

[4] Thomsen, S. F. (2015). Genetics of asthma: an introduction for the clinician. European Clinical Respiratory Journal, 2. https://doi.org/10.3402/ecrj.v2.24643

[5] Why are all snowflakes unique? (2019, January). BBC Bitesize. https://www.bbc.co.uk/bitesize/articles/zmqmrj6

Healthy People Have Beautiful Faces & Disproportion Leads to Ill Health

[1] Hang, D. (2017, April 25). Snoring & obstructive sleep apnea - Happy golden years or a noxious hang over? [LinkedIn post]. Retrieved from https://www.linkedin.com/pulse/snoring-obstructive-sleep-apnea-happy-golden-years-hang-dds-msd

[2] Hang, W. M. (2006). How many years must a profession exist...? CRANIO®, 24(2), 73-75. https://doi.org/10.1179/crn.2006.012

[3] Society for General Microbiology. (2008, November 29). Stomach ulcer bug causes bad breath. ScienceDaily. https://www.sciencedaily.com/releases/2008/11/081123222846.htm

Defining Facial Beauty

[1] Kobyliansky, E. (1991). Fluctuating asymmetry as a possible measure of developmental homeostasis in humans: a review. Human Biology, 63, 441-466.

[2] Linden, O. E., He, J. K., Morrison, C. S., Sullivan, S. R., & Taylor, H. O. B. (2018). The relationship between age and facial asymmetry. Plastic and Reconstructive Surgery, 142(5), 1145-1152. https://doi.org/10.1097/PRS.0000000000004831

[3] Fiala, V., Třebický, V., Pazhoohi, F., Cinová, P., Bašelková, B., Panďurová, I., Rodrigues, J., Fialová, J., & Havlíček, J. (2021). Facial attractiveness and preference of sexual dimorphism: A comparison across five populations. Evolutionary Human Sciences, 3, e38. https://doi.org/10.1017/ehs.2021.33

[4] Catlin, G. (1870). Shut your mouth... and save your life (4th ed., p. 4). N. Truebner and Co. (Reprinted by Kessinger Publishing, Whitefish, MT).

Find out more at and sign up for my newsletter at:

http://tcarneybowles.com

Made in the USA
Monee, IL
01 July 2025

20361256R00118